COACHING AND FEEDBACK FOR PERFORMANCE

DUKE CORPORATE EDUCATION

COACHING AND FEEDBACK FOR PERFORMANCE

Blair Sheppard • Michael Canning • Liz Mellon
Prinny (Virginia) Anderson • Marla Tuchinsky
Cindy Campbell

Dearborn™
Trade Publishing
A **Kaplan Professional** Company

This publication is designed to provide accurate and authoritative information in regard to the subject matter covered. It is sold with the understanding that the publisher is not engaged in rendering legal, accounting, or other professional service. If legal advice or other expert assistance is required, the services of a competent professional should be sought.

President, Dearborn Publishing: Roy Lipner
Vice President and Publisher: Cynthia A. Zigmund
Acquisitions Editor: Jon Malysiak
Senior Project Editor: Trey Thoelcke
Interior Design: Lucy Jenkins
Cover Design: Design Solutions
Typesetting: Elizabeth Pitts

Published by Dearborn Trade Publishing
A Kaplan Professional Company

Printed in the United States of America

06 07 08 10 9 8 7 6 5 4 3 2 1

Library of Congress Cataloging-in-Publication Data

Coaching and feedback for performance / Duke Corporate Education.
    p.   cm.–(Leading from the center)
   Includes bibliographical references and index.
   ISBN-13: 978-1-4195-1507-1
   1. Employees–Coaching of. I. Duke Corporate Education. II. Series.
HF5549.5.C53C63 2005
658.3'124–dc22
                                                        2005018373

CONTENTS

ACKNOWLEDGMENTS

First and foremost, we want to thank our clients and the many program participants around the globe. We begin our work by listening to our clients and gaining an understanding of their business challenges. Working with talented clients and actively engaging in their challenges across a range of industries and geographies has afforded us the opportunity to learn and develop an informed point of view on these topics. We thank our clients for trusting in our approach and making us part of their team. Hundreds of people at all organizational levels have shared their experiences and challenges, and discussed at length the skills, tools, and mind-sets covered in this book, which has deepened our knowledge and insight about coaching and feedback.

We are also fortunate to have an extensive network of faculty, coaches, facilitators, and partners who believe in our mission and have opted to join in our adventure. Together, we have delivered programs in 37 different countries since we formed in July 2000. We absolutely could not have accomplished what we have and learned what we know without their collaboration.

Many thanks to all of those on the Dearborn team, who continue to provide valuable feedback and guide us each step of the way. Their assistance and patience is much appreciated.

Many members of the Duke CE family were willing to share their experiences, personal stories, and (scarce) time in helping us through this process. We especially thank Liz Mellon and Prinny Anderson for their valuable input. In spite of hectic travel and long days, they managed to find time in the margins to help by reading, editing, and sometimes rewriting our thoughts.

Ryan Stevens worked to help capture our methods and processes into the graphical images included within the book, often working with vague instructions. He did a wonderful job.

As always, we could not have accomplished this without the guidance and assistance of our CEO, Blair Sheppard. He supported this initiative from the outset and, more important, always made time to review our output and guide our thinking. His assistance is without measure. We could not have done it without him.

We've drawn on the insight, experience, and expertise of numerous colleagues here at Duke CE. We hope that the content of this book stimulates your thinking and improves your ability to develop your coaching capabilities.

The *Coaching and Feedback for Performance* team: Michael Canning, Marla Tuchinsky, and Cindy Campbell.

INTRODUCTION

In the past 30 years, they have been repeatedly laid off, outsourced, replaced by information technology (IT) applications, and insulted with such derogatory names as "the cement layer." Their bosses accused them of distorting and disrupting communication in their organizations, and their subordinates accused them of thwarting the subordinates' autonomy and empowerment. Who are "they"? Middle managers, those managing in the middle of the organization.

The notion of the middle of an organization has traditionally conjured up a vertical image depicting managers in the middle of a hierarchy. This image carries with it an arcane perception of those managers as gatekeepers and blockages—controlling and slowing down the natural flow of information or resources up or down. It appears to be simple and linear. Given these images, you might think that middle managers are villainous evildoers who sabotage companies or obstructionist bureaucrats who stand in the way of real work getting done. However, the reality is just the opposite. When performed well, the middle manager role is critical in organizations.

Although over the past several decades the value and stature of middle managers has seen both high and low points, we at Duke Corporate Education believe that managing in the middle of the organization has always been both critically important and personally demanding. As one would expect, the essence of the role—the required mind-set and skill set—has continued to change over time. The need to update both of these dimensions is driven by periodic shifts in such underlying forces as marketplace dynamics, technology, organizational structure, and employee expectations. Now and then, these forces converge to create an inflection point that produces a significant change in how organizations are governed, and what role their managers play.

In the *Leading from the Center* series, we examine some of these primary causes that are shaping what it means to successfully lead from the center in the modern organization. We outline the emerging imperative for middle management in an organization as well as the mind-set, knowledge, and skills required to successfully navigate through the most prevalent challenges that lie ahead.

THE NEW CENTER

There are four powerful and pervasive trends affecting the role that managers in the center of an organization are being asked to assume. These trends—information technology, industry convergence, globalization, and regulations—connect directly to the challenges these managers are facing.

Compared to 20 or 30 years ago, *information technology* has escalated the amount, speed, and availability of data to the point that it has changed the way we work and live. Access to information has shifted more power to our customers and suppliers. They not only have more information, but are directly involved in and interacting with the various processes along the value chain. On a personal level, we now find ourselves connected to other people all the time—cell phones, pagers, Blackberries, and PDAs all reinforce the 24/7 culture. The transition from workweek to weekend and back is less distinct. These micro-transitions happen all day, every day because many of us remain connected all the time.

Industries previously seen as separate are now seeing multiple points of *convergence*. Think about how digital technology has led to a convergence of sound, image, text, computing, and communications. Longstanding industry boundaries and parameters are gone (e.g., cable television companies are in the phone business, electronics companies sell music), and along with them, the basis and nature of competition. The boundaries are blurred. It's clear that new possibilities, opportunities, and directions exist, but it isn't always clear what managers should do. Managers will have to be prepared to adapt; their role is to observe, learn from experience, and set direction dynamically. Layered on top of this is the need to manage a more complex set of relationships—cooperating on Monday, competing on Tuesday, and partnering on Wednesday.

Globalization means that assets are now distributed and configured around the world to serve customers and gain competitive advantage. Even companies that consider themselves local interact with global organizations. There is more reliance on fast-developing regional centers of expertise. For example, computer programming in India and manufacturing in China. This means that middle managers are interacting with and coordinating the efforts of people who live in different cultures, and may be awake while their managers are asleep. The notion of a workday has changed as work straddles time zones. Correspondingly, the nature of leading has changed as partnering with vendors and working in virtual teams across regions becomes more common.

The first three forces are causing shifts in the fourth—the *regulatory environment.*

Many industries are experiencing more regulation, while a few others are experiencing less. In some arenas now experiencing more regulation, there is also a drive for more accountability. Demand for more accountability leads to a greater desire to clarify boundaries and roles. Yet there is more ambiguity as to what the rules are and how best to operationalize them. Consider how, in the wake of Sarbanes-Oxley legislation, U.S. companies and accountants continue to sort through the new requirements, while rail companies in Britain are negotiating which company is responsible for maintaining what stretch of tracks. Middle managers sit where regulations get implemented, and are a critical force in shaping how companies respond to the shifts in the environment.

An additional force adding to the managerial complexity is the shifting demographics in the workforce. An aging workforce is having two effects. One is a loss of knowledge and talent as a large number of Baby Boomers enter retirement. The other is that people are living longer and want to stay active both physically and economically; so, we are also seeing an increased number of older people returning to the workforce, even if in a different field. It will be more common in the future to be managing three different generations of workers, each with its own beliefs, experiences, aspirations, and views of work. Both trends impact the complexity of the manager's challenges.

The connection between strategy development and strategy execution becomes tighter every day; so, people in the middle of the hierarchy who understand the strategy but live near the action become more pivotal and important. It will be up to them to simultaneously manage the communication, coordination, and connections required to translate the strategic direction into action and feedback—what's working and what's not—and continue to dynamically shape the strategy.

In addition to communicating and coordinating more actively up and down in the organization, many of them no doubt now find themselves navigating and managing in a matrix, and as part of one or more networks. Their formal authority may still exist vertically, but their real power to achieve results stems from their ability to work across all levels and boundaries. From the center, they act as integrators, sense makers, and catalysts. As depicted in Figure I.1, you are now in the heart of the action, and central to the future success of the organization. Leading from the center produces new and interesting challenges, tensions, and opportunities.

IF YOU ARE LEADING FROM THE CENTER

If you are a manager in the center today, you have many hats to wear, more balls to juggle, and fewer certainties in your work environment. You have to be adaptive yet provide continuity in your leadership. You need to simultaneously translate strategy, influence and collaborate, lead teams, coach and motivate your people, support innovation, and own the systems and processes—all in the service of getting results. Those in the center need more courage than ever. They are the conscience of their organizations, carrying forth the values. At the same time, they build today's and tomorrow's business success.

Strategy Translator

As a strategy translator, you must first understand the corporate strategy and determine what parts of it your group can best support.

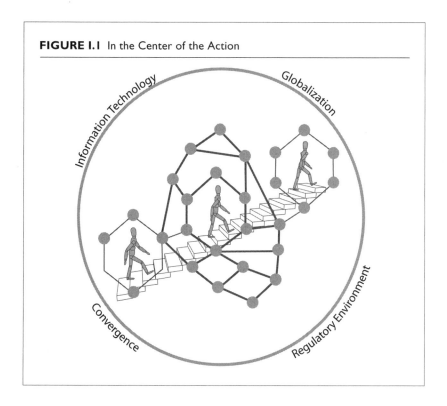

FIGURE I.I In the Center of the Action

Next, you must translate it into an action plan for your group, making sure it aligns well with the overall strategy. You'll need to consider which projects are essential stepping stones and which are needed in their own right, and establish some priorities or guiding goals. You must then communicate the details of the plan and priorities, and create momentum around them. As your team implements, you'll need to involve not only your people but to also collaborate and coordinate with others, including peers, customers, and other units. Instead of directing a one-way downward flow of information, you must translate upward as well and act as a conduit for strategic feedback to the executives above.

Influencer and Collaborator for Results

Middle managers must learn how to make things happen by influencing, integrating, and collaborating across the boundaries of the organization. As a manager, instead of focusing exclusively on your piece, you have to look outside of your own group to develop a network of supporting relationships. Rather than issuing commands and asserting power based on your position, you have to use other tactics to gain agreement and make things happen.

Leader of Teams

Teams have become a one-size-fits-all solution for organizing work in today's economy—virtual teams, project teams, product teams, and function-specific teams—and can be either the blessing or the bane of many companies. Your role as a manager includes understanding the challenges of teams and facilitating their development so that they can be effective more quickly. You have to align the team's energy and talents in a way that will deliver the desired results. You are responsible for creating an environment that will help this group of people work well together to achieve today's objectives and to develop the skills needed to take on future goals.

Coach and Motivator

Although many organizations are well positioned to execute their strategies in yesterday's environment, they are moderately able to meet their current needs and often they are not thinking about how to position themselves for the future. From the center of the organization, middle managers assume much of the responsibility for their people. They create an environment to attract and retain good employees, coach them to do their current jobs better, and bear primary responsibility for developing others. As a manager, you must figure out how to build the next level of capability, protect existing people, connect their aspirations to opportunities for development, and make work more enjoyable. You need to provide regular feedback—both positive and redirecting—and build strong relationships with those who surround you. If done well, your departments will be more efficient and your employees will be better equipped to become leaders in their own right.

Intrapreneur/Innovator

Enabling and supporting an innovative approach within your company will foster the strategic direction of the future. To effectively sponsor innovation, you need to create the context for your people, foster a climate that supports innovative efforts, and actively sponsor the ideas of the future. You have to *be* innovative and *lead* the innovative efforts of others. Innovation is most often associated with new-product development, but innovative approaches also are needed in developing new services or solving internal system and process problems. As a manager, you use their influence and relationships to find the root cause of problems, and the resources to make change happen.

Owner of Systems and Processes

Managers need to understand that part of their role is to take ownership for architecting new systems and processes. You have to shift your thinking from living within existing systems and processes to making sure that those systems and processes work well: Do the systems and processes support or get in the way of progress? One of the mistakes we have made in the past is to not hold managers accountable for their role in architecting the next generation of systems and processes. As a manager, you must perform harsh audits of existing systems, and understand when to tear down what may have been left in place from a past strategy. You need to assess what is no longer relevant and/or is no longer working. Part of your responsibility is to think about and decide whether to reengineer or remove existing systems.

SHIFTS IN MIND-SET NEEDED FOR THE FUTURE

At the end of the day, creating the best solutions and the best results for an organization depends on how its people perform, including you and your team. As performance expectations continue to change and grow, coaching is more critical throughout all levels of a company to help people learn and develop.

Coaching can help people overcome poor performance, develop new skills, learn a newly assigned job, or pursue areas that interest them. Coaching and being coached aren't optional; they're a critical part of your own success, the success of your team, and the success of your company.

Successful coaching depends on a relationship of trust between the coach and coachee, and a supportive environment that stresses that everyone has something to learn and to teach. It also depends on your own competency as a coach. Your ability to successfully coach others is something that you can improve using the models and tips we've included here. Just like those you coach, you will get better with practice and experimentation.

THE CHALLENGE OF COACHING

Picture this: You are a manager, leading from the center of your organization, with responsibility for a diverse team of individuals and several key accounts. Let's meet some of your people.

Amy

Amy, the newest member of your IT support team, is a recent hire from outside the company. She has impressive experience and is remarkably proficient in all the technical areas the team is asked to cover. She's solved a couple of difficult problems already. But there are some indications that she is a poor communicator. When you asked for his feedback, the senior team member noted that Amy tends to respond to clients' questions with one-word answers or overly technical explanations. Internal users report that she sometimes fails to answer their phone calls for help and just shows up at their desks seemingly when she can fit their problem into her work schedule. She devises very efficient plans for the maintenance and upgrade tasks to which she's assigned, but she tends not to let others know about them in advance and often forgets to document her procedures. On occasion, Amy's also forgotten to let you know about her emergency coverage and comp time schedule.

Rasheed

Rasheed is one of the most solid and dependable financial analysts in your group. You feel really lucky to have him and you've started thinking about what else he could be doing. After exemplary performance over the past 1½ years in his current position, you're thinking that he's ready to move into discussing analyses and their implications directly with clients, and he's probably also ready to build his proficiency with some of the more niche products your company offers. You want to make sure that his work continues to be challenging and interesting, and that you understand his future aspirations.

Chris

Chris has been a very successful product specialist for three years, and hasn't expressed any interest in growing beyond that role. He's always demonstrated great skills as a communicator and collaborator, interacting smoothly with other departments, as well as with external vendors, suppliers, and customers. He's well respected among his team members, and seems to be someone they seek out for advice and help. You think Chris has real potential as a leader—and you'd like to have him as a colleague. There are a number of new leadership opportunities opening up in next 6 to 12 months, not just in this area but in strategic locations around the world, that you think he'd be well suited for, but you're not sure that he recognizes his own potential, or that he has considered a future beyond his current department.

Here's what you have: Three unique situations involving three unique individuals with different capabilities, perspectives and aspirations. What do they have in common? First, they are typical of the people and situations that you are likely to encounter as a manager.

Second, they represent the range of opportunities you have to help individuals learn and develop through coaching.

WHY IS COACHING IMPORTANT? WHY DO IT?

"To teach a man how he may learn to grow independently, and for himself, is perhaps the greatest service that one man can do another."
Benjamin Jowett, Vice Chancellor of Oxford University

In today's more complex world of continuous changes in technology, globalization, industry boundaries, regulations, and workforces, ultimately a company's success depends on the performance of its people. Coaching is an imperative for the future success of an organization because it helps people build and hone their skills in ways that make them more effective as individuals, make their teams more effective, and support the organization's strategy and mission. Coaching can help develop the capabilities needed to achieve strategic milestones, develop professionals and leaders for tomorrow, enhance productivity, and improve job satisfaction and retention. Think about the cost—in time, money, and, yes, even frustration—of bringing a new employee up to speed. This may be incentive enough to further develop your coaching skills!

As leaders, you are conveying technical skills and knowledge, but are also modeling acceptable behaviors and values. For many subordinates, their manager *is* the culture. Coaching is a way to demonstrate how your coachee should approach solving problems, interact with clients, work with others, and address personal development.

It's also a personal imperative for the manager-coach and the coachee—both develop and benefit through the experience. People want to do well in their current roles, and they may also have personal aspirations beyond where they are today. It's difficult for them to address these needs alone. Through your coaching, they can learn to do a newly assigned job, overcome poor performance, develop new skills, or move into new levels within the company.

Ultimately, coaching others makes your life as a manager easier. Helping others improve and perform to their capabilities enables them to take on a broader set of tasks, and frees you to do other work and develop your own skills. Coaching makes them better and leverages your time.

WHAT IS COACHING?

Coaching is a developmental partnership, based on the shared responsibility between a coach and an individual. It is not a simple hand-off or transfer of knowledge, but a *relationship* focused on developing people's capabilities. The goal is to instill them with the confidence and skills to aspire to independent achievements, done their own way. Coaching promotes and supports an individual's growth, learning, professional development, and personal benchmarks.

In a typical manager-employee relationship, coaching is an ongoing cycle of goals and desired outcomes, plans, experimental actions, learning opportunities, reflections, and retries that ultimately lead to greater competence. How it occurs can include brief, simple exchanges or more complex, formal interactions.

Successful coaching depends on a trusting relationship and a supportive environment or culture. An organizational culture that supports coaching:

- Is tolerant of people trying (and possibly failing).
- Rewards coaches who perform well.
- Stresses that everyone has something to learn and to teach.

Coaching is related to and may occur in conjunction with managing performance, mentoring, and providing feedback. However, they are not the same.

Performance management is the part of a manager's job that requires the manager to focus on his or her staff's results, on how those results compare to targets, and, if necessary, on correcting behavior or actions. Performance reviews are a time to make sure that the employee clearly understands and agrees on "what to do" during the next quarter or next year. These review meetings can provide an opportunity for coaching, but are not the same as coaching. Performance reviews tend to be more formal, organization driven, periodic, and revolve around standard forms. Ultimately they may be connected to promotions, annual salary increases, or merit bonuses. No wonder managers report that performance management is one of the most stressful parts of their job!

Mentoring is typically broader and longer term, and often a more personal relationship in which the mentor may address the protégé's personal and professional growth. Think of some classic mentors from film and literature: Batman to Robin, Anne Sullivan to Helen Keller, the ghosts to Ebenezer Scrooge, Professor Dumbledore to Harry Potter. These examples typify the nurturing role a mentor plays to a protégé. The focus of mentoring is on the potential and growth of the *individual* first, and on the potential benefits for the organization or team second. Mentors can pass on their knowledge and perhaps open the door to unique opportunities. Mentoring is usually a voluntary and mutually selected relationship, whereas coaching may be a job expectation, or in some cases an expected competency for managers and leaders (Starcevich, 1999). Mentors use many coaching tools, skills, and processes.

Feedback is the information you offer to let people know how well they're doing compared to expectations, how you perceive their performance, and how they're affecting coworkers and customers. Feedback is a necessary *part* of effective coaching, and is critical to people's learning and development outside of coaching as well. When combined with effective coaching, it can help the coachee develop a plan for what to do differently in the future. We'll talk more about skills for giving feedback when we discuss assessing current progress in Chapter 5.

DESIRED OUTCOMES FROM COACHING

Consider some reasons why someone may receive coaching.

- *Coaching for underperformance.* Helps people with problems related to ineffectiveness or poor results.
- *Coaching for enhanced performance.* Builds up someone by adding new knowledge, skills, or confidence—someone who is doing well in his or her current job and can do even better.
- *Coaching for stretch or future performance.* Develops the competencies or characteristics the coachee will need for a future

role; or helps the coachee see his or her talents and potential in new ways. The impetus may come from personal aspirations or from change within the company that requires new competencies.

These types of coaching situations call for slightly different approaches to the coaching process, skills, and techniques we describe here, but the desired outcome in each case is learning and the development of the individual.

THE MANAGER'S ROLE AS COACH

"I start with the premise that the function of leadership is to produce more leaders, not more followers."
Ralph Nader, author

As a manager, you assume many roles. Some roles, such as being a coach, allow you to accomplish several tasks at once. For example, when you coach you help others develop and grow, but you also reinforce the organization's values and culture; you extend the company's capabilities and resources; and, you may build your own reputation and social capital.

Getting Past the Uncertainties

Even when managers and organizations recognize the potential benefits, coaching continues to be a largely underdeveloped and underused tool. The authors of *Getting It Done* describe a situation in which we observe someone and think, "he's making a big mistake," but we hesitate to get involved. We don't point out the good or bad, the mistakes or the good practices. The result is that we miss opportunities to learn or support one another. (Fisher & Sharp, 1998)

Many managers are inhibited when it comes to coaching others. Their reluctance can stem from a variety of reasons. For example, they:

- Aren't aware that it is a key part of their role.
- Don't think of coaching as a tool appropriate to a given situation.

- Don't really understand how to do it, how to begin, what the process is.
- Worry about how much time and energy it will take.
- Doubt whether others actually *want* them to do it—others could view it as a personal attack.
- Are afraid that it could damage their relationship, especially if it's not well received or doesn't go well.
- Believe that coaching isn't rewarded by the organization.
- Don't realize that they already do it and could easily learn to do it more effectively.

These are all valid issues and concerns for you as a developing coach. Throughout this book, though, we offer help to address these issues. Coaching is a *competency* made up of a process, techniques, mind-sets, and skills that you can learn. Just like any other competency that you have acquired throughout your career, your ability to successfully coach others is something that you can develop using the models and tips we've included here. The learning process is dynamic and ongoing, and you will get better with practice and experimentation. The key, to quote the Nike motto, is to "just do it."

GUIDING PRINCIPLES

Although you coach people all around you, in this book we focus on you coaching your direct reports.

In addition to the coaching techniques and tools that we will outline, there are some underlying principles that are critical to your success as a coach. They serve as the basis for all that will follow, so let's introduce them here.

- *The relationship is the foundation.* Coaching requires honest conversation, inquiry, feedback, and a shared responsibility for the outcomes. Because the subject of the conversation is the coachee and coach, it is by definition a more personal interaction than most other conversations in the business setting. This means that progressively building a productive relationship is critical to the quality of the interactions and results. Think about the relationship as a container for the interaction.

As you strengthen the container you can broaden and deepen the conversation and the results that are possible. As a manager-coach, your intentions and actions set the stage and create the conditions to build the container over time.

- *The goal is learning and self-sufficiency.* The purpose in coaching is to expand the other person's confidence, capability, and sense of control. Among the most important yet often overlooked factors for the quality of both the coaching relationship and the results achieved are your intentions and orientation. You have to want coachees to succeed and excel, or you can unintentionally create conditions that will set them up to fail. It's critical that you as manager-coach hold a positive attitude about your coachee's potential and a sincere desire for your coachee to succeed. This is important for two reasons. First, intentions affect your thinking and thinking shapes your actions. Second, intentions "leak." You may think that you have your doubts safely shielded, but they show in nonverbal behaviors, the language you use, what you notice, and the feedback you provide. Your expectations about what you think your coachees can do will color the coaching relationship and results. As you prepare for or are engaged in a coaching interaction, practice performing a fast self-check regarding your intention and attitude. It's the quickest way to positively shape the interaction and ongoing relationship.
- *It's a joint effort.* As a coach, it's your job to create the *conditions* for success—creating the container, guiding the conversation, supplying the necessary resources, enabling safe experimentation, providing feedback, and supporting the coachee's efforts. On the other hand, your coachee is responsible for being open, and acting on the goals, feedback, and support.
- *Keep the right focus.* Coaching in the work context should be focused on the behaviors that affect the coachee's or other people's performance at work. It should not focus on personal attributes, characteristics, or a background that you personally might find less desirable or even annoying. The focus is on work-related behaviors. That said, you may encounter a situation where you surmise that there are behaviors people are engaging in outside work that are negatively affecting their work

performance. Ask for help and guidance from human resources professionals or from more experienced managers about whether or how to deal with these sorts of issues.

- *Get started.* You may be apprehensive about your coaching skills, and about how people will rate or respond to your efforts. Two things to consider: first, *hope is not a good strategy.* Rarely will wishing something to happen make it so in the business world. More important, we've done research with our clients asking what makes coaching valuable within companies. The answer: *to make a difference–it doesn't have to be done perfectly; it just has to be done in a sincere, professional way.*

So, remember the guiding principles and let's get started.

PREPARING TO BE A GOOD COACH

One of your responsibilities as a manager is to get work done through other people. To do that well, you must help your people perform ably and meet the company's goals and their aspirations. As we have said, a key tool for managers is coaching—being coached themselves and coaching their people. Given that being a coach is central to your role, how do you prepare to be a good coach? In this chapter we discuss four fundamentals to being a good coach: *building a relationship with the coachee, being accessible, being competent,* and *being other-oriented.* In other words, be around and approachable, have something valuable to share, and be concerned for the other person.

FORM A COACHING RELATIONSHIP

In each of the challenges addressed in the Leading from the Center series, we propose that building relationships is a critical element to getting results. It is through our relationships that we get work done. Successful coaching—the ability to both give and receive coaching—fits this concept. It depends on the two people (the one providing coaching and the one receiving it) establishing a collaborative working relationship. It's not necessary that they establish a personal relationship or become close friends, but they do need to respect one another and develop a level of trust that allows for clear communication.

Consider what you know about the relationships that exist between the manager (you!) and the employees we introduced in Chapter 1. You have been Chris's manager for three years and consider your relationship well established. He occasionally drops by just to chat about how things are going. Rasheed has been assigned to your team for well over a year, and you consider it a good working relationship. He's one of your most dedicated and dependable staff, and a little more reserved than Chris. You are not sure about his future aspirations. He doesn't tend to initiate conversations, but waits for you to do that. As for Amy, you have only worked with her for a few months and have not really developed your working relationship. There are some early indications that she is struggling, and you need to act quickly to see what you can do to help. You have a slightly different starting point with each coachee in terms of your relationship, but you need to establish relationships that reinforce both a coaching mind-set and a coaching culture that will enable your efforts.

- *Coach's mind-set:* "I'm here to help you grow and work more independently." A coach offers empathy and understanding for the coachee's situation and supports efforts to learn and improve, with a focus on future performance and results.
- *Coaching culture:* "Giving and receiving coaching is part of what we do." Coaching is not provided as a punishment, as micromanagement, or as a sign of incompetence. Coaching helps a coachee improve and develop in his or her current role or get ready for the next role; and *everyone* can benefit from coaching. Remember, King Arthur had Merlin, and Alexander the Great wouldn't have been so great without Aristotle.

Relationships begin by communicating and establishing trust. Social scientists have done extensive research on relationship formation—

Linking Expectations to Outcomes

Your mind-set affects the coaching relationship and the results the coachee can achieve. You set the tone and expectations for what is possible. In a now-famous study of classroom teachers (Rosenthal and Jacobson, 1968), the teachers were told that some of their students were late-bloomers who, with guidance, would excel. By year end, those students had, in fact, excelled—impressive considering they had been randomly chosen and were no different at the start than their classmates. It was *how the teachers treated them* that made the difference. Verified many times over, this "Pygmalion effect" or self-fulfilling prophecy is powerful (Fiske and Taylor, 1991).

What behaviors and reactions are the critical links between expectations and outcomes?

- *Climate.* Create a supportive setting.

- *Feedback.* Be specific in both positive and negative comments.

- *Input.* Teach more difficult or additional information and skills.

- *Output.* Create more chances to produce outputs or to interact (and to get feedback as a result).

In short, your coaching behaviors—verbal and nonverbal—as well as the local culture, will influence your coachee's results.

how we go from being strangers to having a relationship. We begin by exchanging information and going through a discovery process. For example, you might seek to learn more about an employee's unique knowledge, talents, or aspirations. Ask questions. Share a funny story. Go to lunch with the person. Each of you should begin to get a sense of who the other is.

Early in most relationships, people begin negotiating and testing their relationship. These tests are critical—people are implicitly asking, *"Can I trust you? If so, with what?"* Over time, people learn in what ways they can trust each other, and what the boundaries are to their relationship. Boundaries and levels of trust shift over time, and each interaction can have an impact on both.

Some relationships will develop quickly, some more slowly. Not all need to or will reach the highest levels of trust that exist in your strongest relationships, but all do need a basic level of trust to make coaching possible.

The Trust Equation

Maister, Green, and Galford (2000) have developed the Trust Equation to explain the key factors that determine trust levels in any relationship:

$$\text{Trust} = \frac{\text{Credibility} + \text{Reliability} + \text{Intimacy}}{\text{Self-orientation}}$$

Credibility is a mix of how accurately you give information and how honest and forthcoming you seem.

Reliability is the extent to which you do what you say you will do in the time you promised.

Intimacy refers to the comfort level you create for discussing difficult topics, like budgets, layoffs, mergers, and personnel problems. It also includes the level to which you can identify or empathize with the coachee's situation and efforts, perhaps having experienced some of those problems or difficulties yourself.

Self-orientation relates to the balance you maintain between your level of personal motivation—your own interests and agenda—and the level of concern and focus you have for the other person. If you are only centered on yourself, others won't trust you as a coach. People need to feel that you are working for *their* interests, not exclusively for your own or for those of the company.

To increase trust levels, improve the three variables on the top part of the equation and reduce your level of self-orientation.

Without trust, it's difficult to be an effective coach, because coaching is about supporting someone's learning as he or she tries a new skill, gets feedback, and tries again. Coachees have to trust that you will be supportive and fair, and protect the confidentiality of the coaching relationship; otherwise they may not take the risks that lead to learning and improved results. They may second-guess your intentions, question whether they can rely on the information you share, and wonder if you will hold failed experiments against them. Invest in building goodwill, so your coachees believe you're on their side.

BE ACCESSIBLE

It's hard to coach someone if you never interact. You should find ways to make yourself accessible. Being around and being approachable allow you to do two things. First, you can observe firsthand how the person is doing. Second, you can create the space and opportunity for discussions. If you are rarely around or rarely in contact, your coachee may hesitate to bring up anything that isn't closely related to the task at hand. As a coach, you must make it easy for someone to ask for help, share a concern, ask for feedback, or be seen.

A busy manager knew one of her people was going through a rough patch in adjusting to a new role. She herself had been overwhelmed and away from the office more than usual. As a consequence, her coachee muddled along, trying to do his best, but was getting discouraged. She invited him on a visit to the customer, and over dinner apologized for not being around. She explained that she'd asked him along so they would have a chance to talk. Although she had to "manufacture" the access, the coach knew it was important to reconnect and encourage her coachee to reach out to her. "Just because I'm out of the office doesn't mean I'm not available to you." They had a positive discussion, and agreed on how to stay in closer contact.

BE COMPETENT

Would you ask a real estate agent for advice on performing open-heart surgery? Have your favorite auto mechanic plan your wedding? Get legal advice from a landscape designer? Chances are you would match your needs to the person best able to help. Similarly, your coachee is looking for advice from an expert. To prepare yourself to coach well, you have to be valuable to others. You have to invest in yourself, so you can be a useful resource for others.

Part of being a good resource is understanding the skills needed to perform well in your organization, and in particular roles. That means having a broader knowledge about your company and its industry, about your customers and their needs, about developing trends and how they might affect your business. To be a good coach, then, you have to be a good student. You need to keep abreast regularly of the news and developments in your field and industry, and keep your own skills and technical knowledge up to date. Go to conferences, read trade journals, go to local professional group meetings, talk to your customers, and stay in touch with colleagues outside your company. That said, at the end of the day, you can't know everything—also know how and where to get help.

Finally, don't forget to ask your boss or mentor for coaching. As one of our clients puts it, "Coach and be coached."

BE OTHER ORIENTED

Your focus should be on helping the other person learn and grow. You achieve when your coachee achieves. As you prepare to coach someone else, you must keep that person's needs in the forefront. Put your ego aside and think about how best to assist the coachee. People generally know when someone is being insincere or trying to manipulate them. Clearly, this behavior does not build trust!

Think about your favorite athlete. Who coached that person to his or her first really big accomplishment? Can you name the science teacher who got Albert Einstein excited about physics or who helped Jonas Salk work out the polio vaccine? When Nelson Mandela or

Aung San Suu Kyi need advice or help problem-solving, whom do they call? In each case, these people had (or have) coaches behind them, coaches who knew that their role was to help the coachee excel, not to take credit and the spotlight for themselves. Remember the trust equation: as your self-interest increases relative to your interest in the other person's needs, the level of trust declines.

CHECKLIST

❑ What current coaching opportunities exist within your group?

❑ Before you begin, assess your starting points in terms of:
  • Your own coaching mind-set
  • The coaching culture within which you work
  • Your relationship with the coachee

❑ What shifts in mind-set, culture, or relationship would be helpful? What is possible?

❑ Do you make yourself accessible—spending time, being around, being open and approachable?

❑ Have you continued to invest in your own development?

❑ Are you genuinely interested in helping your coachee?

GAPS
A Coaching Process Model

GAPS
A Basic Model

Coaching is about helping someone learn, and the coaching process should reinforce that end. Many coaching models have similar steps. In all cases, the intent is to structure the process, so both the coach and coachee know what to expect. The coaching model we're presenting, as seen in Figure 3.1, is known by the acronym GAPS: Goal Setting, Assessment, Planning, and Support.

GAPS is *a guiding framework*. It is intended to provide basic understanding and guidance; it isn't meant to be restrictive, or taken in a purely literal and linear way. Each coaching situation is different—recall the types of coaching and desired outcomes that we outlined in Chapter 1. You won't always begin at the same step in the process and you won't always spend the same amount of time at each step. Also, not every step in the process will require a separate conversation. You may have quick coachable moments that touch all four

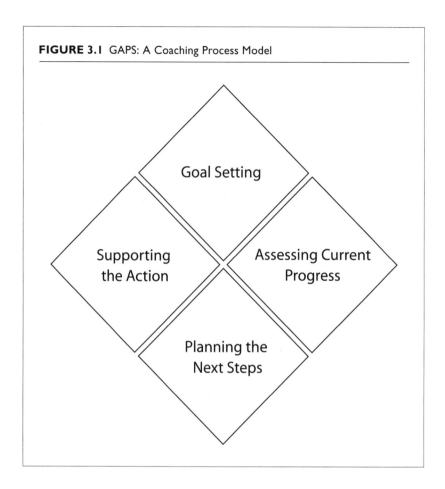

FIGURE 3.1 GAPS: A Coaching Process Model

components of the model. Other times, a more complex coaching opportunity may require a separate conversation at each step to allow the coach and coachee more time to reflect and consider key questions between phases.

Think of the GAPS model as a set of four building blocks that can be assembled in many combinations. With each coachee, the blocks will take a unique form.

GAPS can also be *a planning tool* for managers and for their staff members. You need to think about what your team needs to accomplish and keep it aligned with the overall strategy. Think about who on your team is doing what, what capabilities your team needs to develop, and how your team will get them. (See our books on *Translating Strategy into Action* and *Building Effective Teams* for more detail on assessing and building capability.) As someone who is also learning and developing, you should consider what existing skills you need to improve or what additional skills you ought to develop as you go forward. Place yourself in the role of someone receiving coaching as well.

Goal Setting

Set clear and agreed to goals, such as, what is the coachee expecting to do and by when. Part of this conversation should include why—why *these* goals for *this* person. Part of it should set out how coaching will help the person meet these goals. You should embed learning and improving in the goals. Also remember that goals should be aligned to strategy, that is, what the individual and team needs to do to help the organization achieve its strategic aims.

Assessing Current Progress

Assess how the person is currently doing—what has happened and what progress the person is making toward goals and why. At this stage, the coach and the coachee are jointly gathering data and assessing performance. If progress is on track, the coach should give positive reinforcement. If there is a gap between the goal and current performance, the coach and the coachee should begin by analyzing underlying causes so they can address them.

Planning the Next Steps

Together decide on the next steps to reach the coachee's goals. If progress is on track, you might discuss whether the goals should change or whether you might offer more support. If progress is not on track, then brainstorm alternative strategies for addressing the causes of the lack of progress. The coachee and coach should agree to a plan of action, the timing, and the support the person needs.

Supporting the Action

During all phases of coaching, the coach supports the coachee's efforts in multiple ways.

- Helping set routines
- Checking in periodically
- Providing needed resources and assistance
- Teaching or modeling the behavior or skill
- Giving feedback
- Removing obstacles
- Matching the individual with another coach or expert when needed

As we explore the GAPS coaching model in greater detail over the next four chapters, keep in mind that learning is an iterative process and coaching is an ongoing activity. People take time to develop skills, and generally cannot be experts after one try. Support your coachee through all stages of learning—setting a goal, trying and experimenting, reflecting, and trying again.

CONTRACTING
Agree on the Coaching Need

The coach and coachee should be very clear that coaching is taking place (or is going to take place)—specifically, why and how the two of you will work together. In coaching, this clarification is called *contracting.* Contracting happens at two levels: There's agreement to have a coaching relationship or to pursue some coaching related to a specific need or issue. There's also agreement for a specific conversation. This helps build trust in the relationship—the other person doesn't feel tricked into being coached nor is blindsided by an interaction. Creating this agreement enables you as a coach to easily take advantage of coachable moments when they occur, without awkwardness or fear that your assistance won't be well received.

When you contract for coaching, you talk about the situation, the goals, the roles of the coach and the coachee, and the time frame. As part of this conversation, reinforce the coaching mind-set (you are there to help) and the culture (it's part of their learning and development). For example, with Rasheed who is ready to expand his skills and his role as a financial analyst, the conversation would explore his interest, talk about how you might help him, and reach agreement to proceed. With Amy, who has some communication challenges that are affecting her performance, the conversation may reinforce that everyone has something to learn, and that part of your role is to help people improve.

Agreement for a specific conversation includes stating what you're going to talk about, how long you'll be talking, and possibly whether other people need to be brought in for additional insight or expertise. After you and Rasheed have agreed to coaching for his development, you might proceed to discussing specific goals by saying something like, "Let's talk more specifically for a minute about the new aspects of the analyst role that interest you, and then see how well your current skills and experience match the role. You might also want to talk to a couple of the more experienced analysts to get their perspective on what's involved in their work. Does that make sense?" Be clear about how you view his opportunity for learning and the scope or boundaries of coaching; don't create misleading expectations such as, "success in this area will earn you a promotion."

Contracting may happen in a separate conversation, or it may be part of a larger coaching conversation. Sometimes it's a formal process, especially when more time or greater accountability are involved. It may also be a few informal words early in a conversation to ensure that this is the right time to talk. It may be as simple as asking if the person wants help or advice now on such-and-such task. Possibly, it may be a formal discussion where you and your coachee plan a development program. Contracting is a way to be clear and express joint purpose.

The coach often takes the lead; the coach makes sure that he or she and the other person understand why they are having a particular conversation and what the expectations are. If they don't reach a shared understanding, it can result in confusion or frustration. For example, imagine Greg, who is seen as a rock-solid, down to earth, always knows what to do next. People often come to him for advice. Anna is one of the people who uses Greg as a sounding board. Generally, she approaches him after she has worked through a situation and wants to explore solutions. However, once she approached him just wanting to vent, to share her exasperation about what had just happened. Greg immediately went into problem solving mode. Anna got angry. Why? Because she had different expectations for the conversation than Greg did. They hadn't contracted, so they were having two different conversations.

In some cases, you may be able to readily observe the need for coaching. In other cases, someone may approach you and ask for help. When problems are present, as in Amy's case, concerned colleagues or team members may bring the need to your attention. However the opportunity presents itself, consider the potential benefits from coaching.

Consider how to begin the coaching relationship with Amy, Rasheed, and Chris. Your aim is to agree that coaching is going to be taking place, why (the opportunity), and how you would like to work together.

USE COACHING OPPORTUNITIES

Just as not all coaching is designed to address performance issues, not all coaching will take place in formal and structured settings. Figure 3.2 outlines a spectrum of coaching opportunities that vary in *time, formality, and complexity.*

We may associate coaching with planned sessions between a manager and an employee; however, it is just as effective in brief, focused learning opportunities—or coachable moments across a variety of work relationships. A *coachable moment* is any situation where the coachee is likely to welcome and benefit from coaching at that point. Your days are filled with spontaneous conversations—meet the person in the coffee room, share an elevator ride, stop by en route to a meeting, and so on. These exchanges provide the perfect "excuse" to offer a bit of coaching, continue to build or maintain your relationships, or be accessible in case your coachee wants to chat. You can use GAPS in brief discussions, too. You and the coachee may quickly assess an issue or compare performance against a standard or goal, and you may offer advice or pose a question that helps the person see the situation differently, then plan to check in again.

FIGURE 3.2 Spectrum of Coaching Opportunities

Informal		Formal
Coachable moments	Regular check-ins	Scheduled
Short/focused	Progress updates	Career
Opportunistic	Ongoing feedback	Longer sessions
	Trouble-shooting	Execute over time
	Problem-solving	

Even if the interaction lasts only a few minutes, the learning can be put to use right away. Every day is full of potential coachable moments when something happens that creates an opportunity for learning. Be alert and watchful, notice the opportunities and use some of them for a quick bit of coaching.

Reprinted with permission of King Features Syndicate.

Even though effective, don't rely solely on coachable moments to present themselves serendipitously. Scheduling dedicated time (even if it's only 15 minutes) with your coachee demonstrates that coaching is important and gives you an opportunity to check in. You may not have a set agenda, but instead may chat about progress, give feedback on learning thus far, or discuss any problems that have surfaced. Left unchecked, minor issues can become more complex, so schedule regular times for quick check-ins. You might then schedule lengthier sessions for further coaching, addressing more complex problems, or planning future skill development. Setting aside a longer meeting time for you and the coachee enables both of you to better plan what you'd like to accomplish and have a more focused conversation.

Don't "Overcoach"

Leverage your coaching opportunities—select those that can have the most impact for the individual and for the company. Don't try to explore every possible coaching opportunity for every individual. Evaluate the opportunity and select those that provide the best environment for learning and offer the most leverage. A person who is receptive to your input is more likely to act on it than if it comes as an intrusion or felt criticism. Some signs that someone may be in a coachable moment:

- The person asks for help.
- The person appears apprehensive, frustrated, or anxious.
- The person is about to start something new.
- There are noticeable gaps in performance.
- The person's actions are affecting others.
- You see two people debating or struggling with the right way to do something.

For example, you might seize a coachable moment with Amy at the end of a meeting by asking her to take the lead in communicating to the users the plans that were discussed. Rasheed indicates it's a good time for coaching on enhancing his performance when he volunteers for a new assignment during a team meeting on next year's goals. Chris might signal a coachable moment when he asks about managing next year's supplier contracts, giving you a chance to begin exploring his aspirations and possibilities.

IN ADDITION TO COACHING FOR PERFORMANCE

As we've indicated, people often think of coaching within an organization as only being performance and skill-based, but the aim is how you as a manager-coach can help people be more effective in achieving objectives and aspirations. If you can get your people working more effectively, you succeed, too. In that respect, GAPS is a performance model—set goals, measure progress, and support the person going forward.

However, coaching serves other purposes as well. It can help someone discover his or her place or role. It can help someone overcome problems encountered in the organization's systems. It can help someone aspire, dream, and grow beyond the current situation. In that respect, GAPS is a way of ensuring that you coach more broadly—discuss the coachee's aspirations and begin finding opportunities for him or her, support efforts to explore options and try new approaches, periodically assess whether the person's aspirations have shifted, or help create a new plan of attack. Use the process to help people think about possibilities, gain a different perspective, and optimize themselves.

CHECKLIST

- ❏ Have you reviewed the steps in GAPS and reflected on how you might use them?
- ❏ Have you and your coachee contracted?
- ❏ What opportunities (i.e., coachable moments) typically present themselves?
- ❏ What approach will you use to initiate a coaching conversation?

CHAPTER FOUR

GOAL SETTING

IN THIS CHAPTER

Goals and Why We Need Them ▪ The Value of SMART Goals ▪
Looking beyond SMART Goals ▪ Relationships and Conversations

We've talked about a variety of situations where coaching is an appropriate approach—for example, to help underperformers improve performance, to enhance and grow good performers, and to stretch people's aspirations or performance to new levels. We also talked about the need for contracting, to agree that coaching is taking place and for what purpose, and to focus your coachee. Wherever the coaching conversation begins—with setting goals, assessing progress, planning next steps, or supporting the coachee's efforts—it should define the opportunity for learning, growth, and the outcomes your coachee is working toward.

Even if you and the coachee have a shared view of the opportunities for learning, you may have different views about how the coachee needs to proceed or what to do first. Especially when coaching around performance issues, setting *specific* goals will help you reach shared agreement about what the coachee is striving to achieve. In some cases, you may begin the coaching conversation by

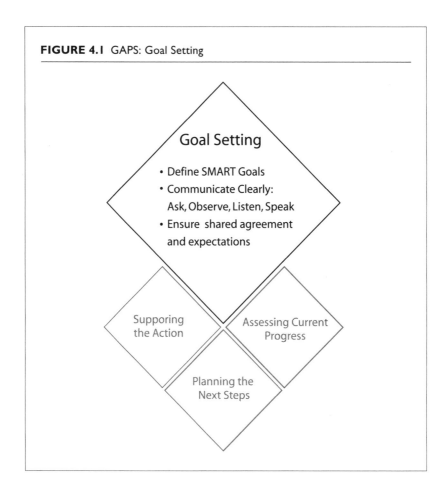

FIGURE 4.1 GAPS: Goal Setting

Goal Setting

- Define SMART Goals
- Communicate Clearly:
  Ask, Observe, Listen, Speak
- Ensure shared agreement
  and expectations

Supporing
the Action

Assessing Current
Progress

Planning the
Next Steps

setting goals; in others you may work toward setting goals after assessing current progress or envisioning future options.

GOALS AND WHY WE NEED THEM

What are goals and why do we need them? Goals define where we want to go and the results that we want from our efforts. When there are competing forces, they help focus our attention and channel our energy toward the most important things.

Goals can drive action at multiple levels—for the organization, for specific divisions or functional units, for teams, and for individuals. Ideally, the goals and aspirations that individuals have are aligned with the opportunities and priorities of their teams and the larger organization. This alignment helps individuals understand where they can play a key role, where the benefits of their efforts will be realized, and how their goals and work are part of a larger purpose.

The vision of outcomes and results that a coachee has in mind will not be achieved overnight, but in stages and through sequenced milestones. People's aspirations may vary widely in span and scope—from being a specialist, to leading a client team, to heading up the new European office, to leading the company. Regardless of the span or scope of their aspirations, coachees should define their goals so that they can set stages and milestones for themselves, and so that their coach knows how to help them.

Creating incremental goals breaks a broader, longer-term outcome into manageable pieces, which helps the person focus and channel his or her energy and attention. Having incremental goals also enables the coachee to experience early successes and maintain forward momentum. For example, if a coachee's vision is to lead client presentations, a key step is enhancing public speaking skills. A first goal might be to complete a one-day public speaking seminar and then to present a brief project update to the team. Each successful attempt or experiment opens the door for a slightly higher goal and a next attempt. The coachee might then move on to presenting a project update to a larger group of people or including more stories or presenting more complex information. But the first goal or attempt would certainly not be to present at a national industry conference.

THE VALUE OF SMART GOALS

People often have trouble meeting their goals not because they aren't trying, but because they haven't given their goals enough definition. Starting with goals that are vague, unrealistic, too broad, difficult to measure, or lacking a target completion timeline puts people at a disadvantage. If they are unsure what to do, how to do it, or by when, how can they possibly succeed?

When coach and coachee are focusing on performance issues, creating SMART goals can help provide enough definition to get the coachee started, and enable you to assess progress and better ensure success. What characteristics do SMART goals have? Depending on the definition you prefer, they are specific, measurable, attainable, action-oriented, agreed on, achievable, attractive, realistic, relevant, trackable, timely, and tangible.

SMART goals should be:

- *Specific and positively stated.* Both of you should understand what the desired outcome is (what to *do* rather than what *not* to do), what challenges or barriers might occur, and what support will be available.
- *Measurable and observable.* Both of you must understand how and when you will gauge learning, progress, and success using measures that are as objective as possible. Defining a "floor" and "ceiling" range of outcomes can provide challenge to the coachee while mitigating stress.
- *Actionable and agreed on.* The goals must be ones the coachee can act on. You both need to understand what's involved and agree on how to proceed.
- *Realistic and challenging.* The goal may be hard but it's something that you both agree this person can actually accomplish. The goal (especially the most immediate goal) may not be the ultimate vision, but is one step or one level of learning towards achieving the ultimate vision.
- *Time-bound and documented.* Creating time targets provides structure, helps keep the coachee moving forward, and enhances clarity and accountability. With no deadlines, a learning or development effort can go on indefinitely, and progress or achievement is hard to measure. Create a record of the goals for future reference and shared clarity.

Most important, the goals that you and your coachee create as part of the coaching process need to be relevant and rewarding for the individual. If the goal is not something the coachee *wants* to accomplish, it will be harder to achieve.

In a coaching situation, the two of you should work together to set goals for the coachee and discuss how you will support his or her actions. Although taking time to write SMART goals and talk through each of the attributes may seem overly formal or even annoying, our experience shows that it truly is a valuable exercise. Resist the urge to bypass this step, as it can reveal if the two of you have different assumptions or expectations, and so avoid problems down the road. For example, if you each have different views of what's realistically achievable in a defined period, it's better to talk it through at the start rather than have the coachee miss the mark later on.

For example, Amy has occasionally forgotten to let you know about her emergency coverage and comp time schedule. You could ask Amy to agree to "communicate with you more," but what does that really mean? Will it get the results that you want? It may be hit or miss if that's all she has to go on. Her definition of "communicate with you" may differ dramatically from your definition. A smarter goal for Amy would be "To notify her manager, via e-mail or voice mail, of her emergency coverage and comp time schedule at least 24 hours in advance of being out of the office."

It's important to establish a relationship that allows you to discuss goals in detail, including the roles you will each play and how these affect the outcomes. For example, you need Amy to let you know in advance so that you have time to arrange coverage without inconveniencing other team members. The coachee *expects* you to be involved, ask questions, and offer advice.

LOOKING BEYOND SMART GOALS

Congratulations!
Today is your day.
You're off to Great Places!
You're off and away.
Dr. Seuss, *Oh, the Places You'll Go!*

The longer-term development outcomes you envision should help guide your approach and emphasis when setting nearer term or interim goals. Setting very specific goals is useful when a manager and direct report are working through performance issues or enhancements, but when coaching shifts toward guiding someone to recognize and visualize what might be accomplished in the future, it's more useful to think in terms of a larger framework.

Aspirational goals have a scope well beyond where coachees are today and challenge them to consider where they want their talents and potential to take them. Aspirational goals should be exciting and stimulating—something they are really motivated and energized about accomplishing. Otherwise, as Dr. Seuss describes, you could end up in "the waiting place" with all the other people who are simply waiting for something to happen to them rather than seeking out the things that will most excite and energize them.

Aspirations are also one piece of the coachee's overall life plan and need to align and integrate with longer term goals for other life domains—friends, family, community, finances, and health. It's important for a manger to be accessible for discussions of careers and larger, longer-term aspirations. This is as much a part of your coaching responsibility as specific performance-oriented goal setting.

Chris is a good example of someone who needs help conceptualizing his goals beyond his current situation. You've asked Chris out to lunch in hopes of learning more about his aspirations and what things are most important in his life at this point. You think he has the potential to develop into a good leader, but you aren't sure whether leadership is something that interests him, whether he has other plans in mind, or whether he needs help in recognizing his own potential as someone who can lead. You begin the conversation by pointing out to Chris that he's really good at a number of key leadership skills.

You:	*Hey Chris, glad you could get out of the office for lunch today. It seems like every time I come by your desk there's a line of people seeking your help. You really communicate well with your team members, and I think they value your input and advice.* • Point out some of Chris's talents he may be unaware of.
Chris:	*Yeah, I've been here awhile, so the new folks especially have figured out that I'm someone who can usually answer their questions. Mostly, they just need a little guidance. I don't mind; I'm happy to help.* • Chris reveals one of the things he likes about his job.
You:	*You also seem to work well with our vendors. You know, those are the same talents that help people develop into good leaders. Is taking on a broader leadership role something you've considered? You seem to have a knack for it.* • Connect talents to possibilities.

RELATIONSHIPS AND CONVERSATIONS

Relationships depend on good communication. The coaching relationship you create needs to allow you and your coachee to have the kinds of open conversations that clarify and explore expectations, goals, and desired outcomes, as well as other issues. Approach all coaching conversations as collaborative, mutual exchanges of ideas and possibilities.

Coaching conversations are not always easy. They may be uncomfortable and challenging for one or both of you, especially if the desired outcome of the coaching is to improve a performance problem. When there is conflict, conversations become even more challenging. The two of you may view an opportunity differently, or one of you may misinterpret something the other said, causing the other to become defensive. How you handle these moments will define the relationship and your ability to work together. A conversation can easily go awry if your emotions or goodwill are exhausted. If the conversation becomes too hard or too negative, it's time to take a break and try a different approach.

Build and maintain goodwill by keeping their learning and growth as your primary goal. Goodwill comes through creating a shared sense of purpose and investment in the future—but *goodwill is built over time.* Take care to protect the relationship even while you have a difficult conversation or work through a conflict.

How good are your conversation skills? How do good conversations work? A good conversation is like a cycling team: the members take turns leading and following over the course of a race. Good conversations include asking, listening, observing, and speaking—and perhaps asking and listening again.

- *Ask questions* to get feedback and to check effect and understanding.
- *Listen* to answers to hear the words and understand their intended message.
- *Speak* to help others understand your views.
- *Observe* to detect clues to the effect and understanding of your words.

When Asking Questions

Ask questions with a genuine desire to see things from other people's points of view: how they view the situation, their goals for learning, or how they have interpreted what you have said. Tips include:

- Ask open-ended questions to explore someone's thinking. If you ask closed questions (i.e., that require only one word answers), you limit the range of responses and imply that you already know the answer. *Why did you respond that way?*
- Ask closed questions to confirm understanding. *Is that what you meant?*
- Ask what-if questions to help spark thought. *What would happen if you tried this instead?*
- Ask for advice rather than giving it. *What do you think should happen?*
- Don't assume you know what the person means.
  - Do ask for clarification when things are unclear.
  - Don't try to finish someone else's sentences.
  - Don't say, "I know just how you feel."
- Check your tone for sincerity. As you talk, does your tone of voice match your feelings and body language? For example, a supervisor can sound angry when he's actually just concerned for his employee.

Match your questions with their purpose.

- To check effect of statements or actions. *I hear you saying you are frstrated with the level of support you've received, is that right?*
- To gain information and insight. *What happened next?* or *How did that make you feel?*
- To focus attention and awareness. *Tell me more about your ideas for the project.*
- To stimulate thinking and self-discovery. *What do you think your options are at this point?*

When Listening

Listening is important in all phases of the coaching relationship, but especially so at the beginning. Really listening is a core element to building rapport and trust.

If either of you enters the conversation with an attitude of already knowing what should happen and with the intent of persuading the other person to that point of view, then you will automatically limit your ability to listen. It's critical not only that you *are listening* but also that you demonstrate to the other person that you are listening and considering what you hear.

There are specific actions that you can take in different situations to enhance listening and understanding.

- *Seek the other person's views and be prepared to listen* without thinking of what you want to say next, thinking of other unrelated topics or events, or projecting your own feelings and ideas onto the other person.
- *Check your understanding* by paraphrasing what the other person says and checking that you heard correctly by asking, "Is that what you mean?" and by verifying that you have heard all that the person wanted to say by asking, "Is there more that you want to say?"
- *Show you recognize the importance of the other person's views* by validating that person's reactions and understanding of things.
- *Show that you are concerned with the other's welfare* by empathizing with the feelings and needs behind what the person has said; for example, ask, "Are you feeling _____ because you are needing _____ ?"

Let's return to your conversation with Chris. During your lunch, you tried to help him make the connection between his innate talents and the skills needed for good leadership. You gave Chris some options to consider without pressing the point. A week later, you continue the conversation in your office, and Chris quickly indicates he's not sure if he has what it takes to move to a leadership role. You ask him to consider what qualities he thinks a leader should have.

| Chris: | *I guess you have to have expertise in the area you're leading–like industry knowledge. Also management skills–like motivating people, communicating well, knowing when to delegate, and being available.* | • Analysis |
| You: | *Do you realize that you already have many of these skills, and are well on your way to developing the rest?* | • Guiding question |

Chris:	*I hadn't thought about it that way.*	• Eureka!
You:	*If you're interested, we could explore some areas that you could work on developing further. For example, if you learned more about how the whole company works–other divisions–it could help you see the connections among the parts of the business. I can help you to start building relationships with people in other areas.* *Maybe you could take a basic management skills course to reinforce what you already know? It could give you a new way of looking at some topics.*	• Some potential goals to begin building the foundation
Chris:	*Yeah, that sounds good. How should I get started?*	• Agreeing to coaching and asking for help
You:	*For one thing, I need to assign a representative from our group to serve on a new cross-functional product team. You wouldn't be leading the team, but it would be good exposure to some of the other functions. Why don't you research what management courses are available during times that work for you, and then let me know in a few weeks what you'd like to register for.*	• Goals • Who will do what • Future check-in time

When Speaking

Be sensitive to the situation and the message you are delivering, while ensuring that the intended message has been delivered. When you have to deliver difficult messages, be direct, but also be aware of the effect your words have on the other person and use language that allows him or her to actually hear and take in the difficult message. That may mean using terminology familiar to the listener, slowing down the pace, or making the language as neutral and clear as possible.

One common source of difficulty in getting your message across the way you intend is that words often have different meanings depending on context or organizational culture. For example, do the two of you share a common understanding of words like *problem, timely, own,* as well as of words that are slang or jargon?

When Observing

Multiple nonverbal communication modes are used during conversations, beyond the actual spoken words. Those nonverbal modes are important to the flow of the conversation and they can signal how well your intended message is being received and interpreted. Typical nonverbal communications come from the amount of eye contact, your facial expressions, and your body movement. The person you are speaking with will also send nonverbal messages.

Figure 4.2 offers some examples of nonverbal communicators. What different messages do they send? The drawback of nonverbal communication is its ambiguity; a furrowed brow may indicate that I don't agree with what you're saying, or simply that I don't yet understand it.

People send and receive any number of nonverbal cues during a conversation and they interpret those cues within the context of the situation and the individuals involved. Be cognizant of all of the cues you send and make sure they communicate what you intend. For example, for you, tapping a pencil may simply be a nervous habit that you don't notice, but the coachee may interpret it as a signal that you don't want to be part of this conversation and wish it to end soon. Closing your eyes while the coachee is speaking may be your way of paying closer attention, while it may appear to be a signal that you are tired of listening to the coachee talk.

Has your conversation had the outcome you intended? When you speak, you know what you intend, but the other person perceives and interprets may be something altogether different. Sometimes, the communication goes wrong, and your intended message has an unintended impact. What could have caused this? The problem may be that a word means one thing to the speaker and something completely different to the listener.

At the conversational level, how can you each ensure that you are hearing the message that the other intended? If it feels like the conversation isn't flowing, if you think the other person might not understand, or if the person is getting upset, pause, ask questions, and listen completely to the answers. If you have offended or upset the other person, apologize and ask to try again.

FIGURE 4.2 Nonverbal Communicators

Tone and Clarity of Voice	Conversational tone, formal tone, raised voice, soft voice, mumbling, sighs, clear enunciation, rapid speech, slow speech
Facial Expressions	Raised eyebrows, frowns, smiles, yawns, pursing lips, vacant stares, furrowed brows, rolling eyes
Eye Contact	Direct eye contact, avoiding direct eye contact, closed eyes, looking away, looking down
Gestures/ Movement	Nodding, rubbing jaw or chin, scratching head, rubbing brow, pointing finger, shuffling feet, looking at watch or clock, tapping pencil, shaking head, putting face in hands
Body Posture/ Proximity	Leaning forward, sitting up in chair, leaning away, leaning back in chair, hands behind head, legs crossed, slouching in chair

CHECKLIST

❏ Recall and reinforce the coaching contract and why you started this process.

❏ Begin with the outcomes the coachee is working toward.
  - Work together to define them in terms of SMART goals.
  - Talk through areas where you have different opinions or views.

❏ Use your conversation skills to help gain clarity around the goals.
  - Ask questions.
  - Check your understanding.
  - Listen well.
  - Share your views.

❏ Verify that you have shared agreement on the goals and your roles going forward.
  - The specifics of what the coachee is going to do and when.
  - That you are approachable and available to support her effort.

CHAPTER FIVE

ASSESSING CURRENT PROGRESS

IN THIS CHAPTER

Gathering Data ■ Providing Feedback ■ Exploring "Why?"

Assessing the coachee's current progress and results, and sharing that assessment with the coachee, are key components in coaching the person for improved or enhanced future performance (see Figure 5.1). Some coaching interactions may begin with this step. For example, you might take advantage of a quarterly performance review to begin discussing current progress and performance, before moving on to other aspects, such as setting new goals or future aspirations. In other interactions, you may not discuss current progress until the coachee has had some time to experiment with new skills or previously agreed to goals.

An added benefit of creating SMART goals is that you have clear performance targets in place when it's time to assess progress and results. Also, both of you should already understand how the coachee's learning and progress will be measured and have initial time-based targets. These target dates provide a good opportunity for pausing the action and assessing the coachee's progress and results to that point.

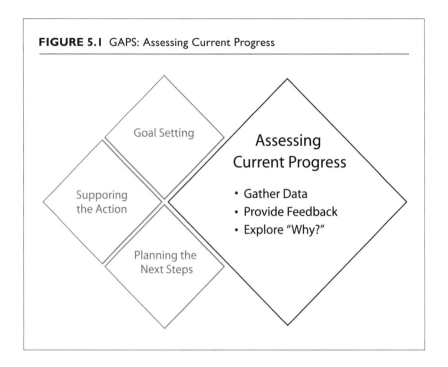

FIGURE 5.1 GAPS: Assessing Current Progress

Goal Setting

Supporing
the Action

Planning the
Next Steps

Assessing
Current Progress

• Gather Data
• Provide Feedback
• Explore "Why?"

GATHERING DATA

As you prepare for a conversation to discuss the coachee's current progress and results, *work from data whenever possible.* Your mental models, previous experiences, and general perceptions are not the same as the coachee's. They put you at a different starting point and may lead you to conclusions about a situation that the data may or may not support. Second, your perceptions of frequency can be skewed. You may *think* that something was most often the case because one instance is memorable; however, when you actually look at the data, you may see that this instance was the exception rather than the norm. Also, if you have observed the coachee on several occasions, you may tend to allow your most recent observation to influence your memory of the others.

If you work primarily from general perceptions, your feedback is likely to be too general as well. Gather enough data so that you can give your coachee specific examples of things that were done well and things that could be improved. "You did a really good job" is nice to hear, but so vague that the person doesn't have any thing specific to use for future reference. It gives the person more to reflect on if you instead say something like, "I really liked how you handled that lost order. You calmly explained to the customer the steps you would be taking and the time line, and then you had a great tone with the shipping group—not accusing them, but asking for their help in sorting through a mix-up. It was really effective."

Collect Data from Multiple Perspectives

Just as you don't rely on general perceptions, don't rely on a single set or a single source of data. The coachee may have had several opportunities to experiment and learn. A single observation or data about how he or she is doing may be accurate but may not be sufficient to work from. As a coach, you must consider your coachee's performance from multiple perspectives. You may discuss and agree in advance as to who would be in the best position to assess the coachee's performance and progress. People in different places at different times pay attention to different things. By getting others to offer data, you get a more complete picture of how and what the coachee is doing. Broader input will help you make a more accurate assessment.

- How does the coachee assess the progress? Self-evaluation asks the coachee to take ownership of his or her learning. Evaluating one's own work and progress is not always straightforward; we all have biases. Ask the coachee some open-ended questions that guide the coachee to make connections between efforts and results achieved. For example, you might use the following questions during your conversation, or in written notes prior to the conversation:
  - Describe the goal that you are working toward.
  - What do you think has gone well?
  - What have you found difficult?
  - What other factors contributed to the outcomes you've gotten?
  - If this isn't the result you wanted, what needs to change, so you can be more successful the next time?

- How do others think the person is doing? Others have observed the amount of learning or progress that the coachee has made. Team members, clients, vendors, and other managers have likely been in positions to observe and evaluate performance. Gather their feedback with questions that:
  - Pertain to the coachee's specific goal, not every possible criterion for success.
  - Assess how well the individual performed during *this* observation (not previous performance).
- How do you think your coachee is doing? Create opportunities to observe both informally (attending a team meeting) and formally (during a client visit). When observing the coachee, you will be more aware of the starting point in the process and the goal toward which the coachee is working. This inside knowledge puts you in the unique position of completing your own assessment, but also of observing the reactions and feedback of others.

PROVIDING FEEDBACK

Once you've gathered and considered data from multiple sources, you will have a better overall picture of how well your coachee is doing, but there are still some things you don't know. The coachee is working primarily from his or her own observations thus far, and you are working from yours. Separately, they are only pieces of a complete picture. Now you have to provide feedback on how you and others view the coachee's current performance and learn more about how he or she is viewing things.

Too often, feedback is associated only with poor performance. Thus people build negative associations with receiving feedback—*someone is going to judge me, criticize me, and tell me all the things I'm doing wrong*—or with giving feedback—*I have to tell them they're not doing a good job and they're going to be upset.* Feedback is actually a critical part of learning and is essential to all levels of performance from positive reinforcement of strong performance and stretch efforts, encouragement and redirection for variable performance, or even more emphatic course correction for lack of results or significant mistakes. *People need to give and get feedback regularly to promote learn-*

ing. All sentient beings need feedback to survive; employees need it to be able to perform up to expectations.

Feedforward versus Feedback

Marshall Goldsmith outlines what he believes is a fundamental problem with all types of feedback: that it focuses on what has already occurred and not on the opportunities for what could happen in the future. Goldsmith describes an alternative, *feedforward,* as giving someone suggestions for the future.

He has observed thousands of leaders in an experimental exercise in which they have an opportunity to both give and receive feedforward. Participants commonly described the exercise as energizing and fun, and he questioned why they saw the exercise as helpful as opposed to embarrassing or uncomfortable. Goldsmith notes that participants' answers give insight as to why feedforward can be more useful than feedback. They made comments such as:

- We can change the future. We can't change the past.

- It can be more productive to help people be "right," than prove they were "wrong."

- People do not take feedforward as personally as feedback.

- Face it! Most of us hate getting negative feedback, and we don't like to give it.

(Goldsmith, 2002)

Giving feedback is also a chance to reinforce the organization's culture, team-level priorities, and individual aspirations and achievements. If an individual's actions are demonstrating the organizational culture—the way that team members should support one another, how problems should be addressed, or how partnerships should work—feedback reinforces those actions and lets others know that it is noticed. If someone is making good individual progress, feedback reinforces that the coachee is on the right track and perhaps sets new challenges. If the individual isn't making good progress, feedback helps the coachee to refocus and re-energize for the next experiment or attempt, with some suggestions of how to do things differently.

Here are some tips for delivering feedback well.

Remember why you are doing this and what's important. Remind yourself (and your coachee if needed) why you are offering coaching and feedback. Use the opportunity to reinforce:

- The coaching relationship
- Your positive intentions
- Learning as the primary goal
- Connections to your coachee's work.

Restate any previous goals as they were originally agreed. Be careful that you don't change or add goals. Effective feedback and coaching are partly about staying focused and not trying to change too much at once. For example, if, as you're observing, you notice a new skill that would also be worthwhile to work on, don't interject it at this point. Let the person complete the learning cycle that you agreed to. Focus on making progress toward *this goal.* You can always discuss the new skill in the next round of coaching.

In general, offer more positive than negative feedback. Let people know what they're doing right, so they keep doing it. *Look for opportunities to positively recognize when a person has demonstrated the desired behaviors and is making progress, even small steps.* Sometimes you need to deliver negative feedback. Take care, however, to avoid delivering "hamburger criticism"—sandwiching the "meat" or negative message between two pieces of praise. (Gaines, 1995) First, it can seem disingenuous. Second, the person may not hear the second positive piece anyway, while still reacting to the negative criticism.

If there is a problem, consider beginning with your positive feedback and then offering suggestions for how the coachee could be "even better if . . ." The person still hears that you'd like to see a change, but it's framed as a positive improvement instead of remedying a deficiency.

Finally, if the feedback is significant and the person needs a real change in behavior, that point alone should be the focus of the conversation. If in this particular instance you need to focus on an area for improvement, then don't artificially inject praise.

Don't delay too long in offering feedback. Feedback is most helpful when "in the moment" or shortly thereafter. The coachee needs to understand how he or she is doing and what adjustments he or she needs to make for the future, and delaying providing feedback also delays her progress. As with other components of coaching, feedback can sometimes be given quickly in a coachable moment. In other situations it may be more appropriate to set aside time to have a conversation about what learning and progress have been achieved thus far by comparing actual results to goals.

Focus on what is important, appropriate, and something the person can or will do something about in the future. Don't overload the coachee with too much; set out what is important and focus the person on that. Similarly, consider whether the feedback is appropriate, and whether it is appropriate for *you* to give it. The most useful feedback addresses actions that someone *can change* and would be *willing to change*. A coachee may be able to do a wide range of tasks, but if he or she's trying to move into a new job, the coachee may not be willing to do more of something that is part of the current job. Behaviors (habits or personality) are not as easily changed as areas such as job skills or approaches to managing work. Suggesting to someone who is a linear, methodical thinker that he or she needs to think more abstractly and metaphorically may be asking for an impossible (and inappropriate) change. The person simply cannot. So, this is not good feedback.

Be specific when describing what you and others are observing. Avoid generalizing or exaggerating. For example, it's more helpful to say "You were 20 minutes late for two critical meetings this week" rather than "you are always late." Be descriptive, and avoid judgmental comments like: "If you'd just get your head out of the clouds you'd be on time for important meetings."

Explain the effects of your coachee's actions. Describe how what you observed *could have* or *did have* an impact on the coachee, other individuals, the team, or the department. For example, if your coachee has a tendency to dominate conversation during meetings, say, "During the client meeting, I could tell that you were making an effort not to interrupt others and to focus your comments. That was an improvement. As a result, several of the group participated more than they have in the past, and their ideas were great. We should be able to come up with several good options for the design. The client was quite happy."

Involve the coachee. The intent of this discussion is not for you to do all the talking, measuring, or assessing of the coachee's learning and progress. The intent is for your coachee to take responsibility for performance *and* for assessment. You want to learn more about how *the coachee* views his or her performance thus far, how the coachee thinks others perceive him or her, how the coachee sees the impact of his or her actions, and finally where the coachee thinks the gaps are. Personal involvement in the assessment will also make it more natural for the coachee to be involved in planning for new or different actions for the future.

Check for indicators that he or she's getting it. Is the feedback being delivered effectively? Ask questions to check how the coachee understood your comments.

Checking In with Amy

You've now observed Amy, your IT support person, on several occasions and have also gathered some data from other team members and users with whom she has interacted. You think Amy is technically very adept but has some challenges with communicating well. It's important to give her feedback now rather than waiting several more months for the next scheduled performance review. You've scheduled a meeting with Amy to give her feedback—some positive and some negative—and learn more about how she views her performance.

You begin the conversation of how things are going for Amy by acknowledging that it can be challenging to start a new job, and you restate that you are here to help and provide feedback. You ask Amy some open-ended questions to learn more about her views of her performance thus far, and how well things are going. Now it's time to give Amy feedback.

You: *Amy, your technical skills are excellent. Your team members were impressed when you solved the security glitch during your first week here. And your plans for the maintenance and upgrade tasks were organized and detailed and helped those projects go well.*

- Be specific about the things that Amy is doing well.

You: *I'd like to help you continue to grow in this position and do well at the company. Based on what I've observed and feedback I've gotten from others, I think that you can become even more effective by improving your communication skills. Do you have any thoughts about that?*

- Goal is to help Amy improve and learn.
- Focus is on future.
- Importance of communication skills.
- Involve coachee.

Amy: *I want to take the lead on update projects in the future. I enjoy that more than direct user support. Will working on my communication skills help me do that?*

- Amy expresses what areas interest her most.

You: *Probably. Let's keep that in mind as a goal for the future and discuss it at your formal review. For now, user support is an important part of your role. Other areas depend on you to keep them functioning and doing their jobs, so it's important to respond to their calls quickly and get them back up and running. A couple of things you can work on:*

   Our department goal is to field all support calls on the first try, even if they interrupt another task. Making a special trip to the user's desk later delays resolving the problem. If possible, you need to field support calls when they occur.

   Our users don't have the technical knowledge that you have, and need simple explanations and directions for their problems. In your conversations with users, sometimes you can be overly technical. Try to avoid using technical jargon and just explain the situation in terms they can understand. Don't give them too much detail.

   Does that feedback make sense to you? What are your thoughts?

- Reinforce that you heard what Amy said.
- Be specific about what needs improvement.
- Show how her actions can impact others.
- Address the most important, immediate problems (user support).
- Avoid too much feedback at one time.
- Check for understanding and keep coachee involved.

Amy: *I understand. I didn't realize I was being too technical. I think I've been so anxious to work on the updates that I sometimes forget to respond to user calls, or I try to speed through my calls with them.*

- Amy confirms that she understands the feedback.

You talk further with Amy about details of the feedback you've just given. Amy conveys her frustration at having demanding tasks "interrupted" by user calls. She also believes that "people who use the system should bother to learn more about how it works." You empathize with her frustration and brainstorm ways to handle scheduling tasks that require steady concentration. You also acknowledge Amy's passion for systems expertise but reiterate that it is part of her job nonetheless to work with the users who are less knowledgeable. You make it clear that she needs to treat users like customers.

You:	*I think you can get the results we both want–quick resolution–with better communication. Give these techniques a try and let's talk again in a few weeks.*	• Amy has some specific things to work on. • You confirm that you are going to follow-up to see how she's doing.
Amy:	*Thanks. I understand and will work on improving both of these things. I'll also try our idea of scheduling some of the tasks that need my full concentration during the low call volume times.*	• Amy agrees to the goals and selects one of the brainstorming ideas.

EXPLORING "WHY?"

As we noted, one of the reasons for gathering data is that you and the coachee may have different starting points and draw different conclusions about the progress. When offering feedback and talking through the details of someone's performance, *exploring why* he or she achieved certain results will often reveal even more details. The better you both understand the connections between actions and results—whether positive or not—the better you will understand how to plan for the future.

If the feedback is positive, make sure that you convey specifically what the coachee did that generated the good results. Then explore how that good performance can build on getting even better at this task or taking on a more challenging goal. In Amy's case, her problem solving skills have already proven valuable to the team, and you make sure that she knows this. You also make it clear that improving her communication can make this good performance even better and you reinforce how communication is an expected element of acceptable team performance and organizational culture.

If the feedback is not positive, the conversation should then be directed toward *why* the desired results were not achieved. During your assessment of progress and results, issues will emerge that you need to consider further. Even if the two of you have a shared assessment of the results, you may not have the same view of why. It's essential to consider the causes before moving forward with a plan on how to approach the task differently. Otherwise, you may just continue getting the same results.

Get to root causes whenever possible when evaluating why something happened as it did. This includes exploring relevant issues both for the coach and for the coachee. Coaching is a partnership; assess how both of you might have contributed to the cause. Often, the root cause is not the first explanation that comes to mind. It may take more exploration, and some questions.

For example, you may believe that Amy uses overly technical terms with system users because she doesn't realize that they don't understand the terminology. You believe that if she were aware of their actual level of knowledge and if she saw them as her "customers," she would switch to using simpler terms and ordinary language. However, Amy uses technical language because she believes that anyone who uses a system should have some depth of knowledge about it. That was the perspective where she last worked. She believes that it's her job to educate users to use the right technical terms—she sees them as the "unenlightened" whom she should be helping. Until you and Amy come to a shared understanding, Amy is less likely to behave differently because she won't understand why it matters and how treating users like customers is a different mind-set.

One popular model of exploring the root cause of a problem is the "Five Whys" method. By asking *why* up to five times, you can work through the layers of reasoning and reveal the root cause of a problem. Begin by writing down the specific problem, and then asking *why* the problem happens. For each answer, ask *why* again. Continue asking and answering (the number of why's isn't really important), until you think you've found the root cause, keeping in mind that there may be multiple causes. (Senge, et al., 1994)

For example, you might ask a coachee why he doesn't speak up in team meetings, and his answer might be, "Everyone else covers the points, so there's no reason for me to repeat what they've said." The second *why* might be something like, "Why is there no value in hearing that you think similarly to the way they do?" The coachee might say, "Well, it's not that important, as long as I go along with their ideas." The third *why* might be just a plain, "Why?" At that point, the coachee might say, "I'm the newest person on the team, and they've already got their set ways of doing things. With this group, it doesn't matter what I think. It's more important to just fit in." The fourth *why* might be phrased, "Why is it more important to just fit in?" As this conversation unfolds, you may begin to recognize an issue in the dynamics of the team that is making it hard for the newest member to suggest new ideas, which would lead you to change the way you conduct the meetings. You might coach the team to elicit ideas from everyone before assuming they have consensus, as well as coaching the new team member to speak up.

The underlying reasons the coachee doesn't get the targeted results might fall into any of the following categories or may be a combination of reasons, rather than a single cause.

Capacity issues. In today's business environment it has become the norm to have multiple, important priorities competing for our time. It may be that some people don't perform as well as hoped because they had too much assigned to them, or that they miscalculated their capacity and signed up for too much, or they didn't manage their time effectively.

For example, in her desire to do well in a new position, Amy may have volunteered for too many of the maintenance and update tasks, not leaving enough time for her share of the regular support calls. Why? Perhaps the importance of the user support part of her position wasn't sufficiently conveyed. Perhaps improving her communication skills will make this a more enjoyable part of her work.

Capability issues. Some people don't reach their targets because they don't have the needed knowledge and skills. In today's rapidly changing business environment even good performers regularly experience capability gaps or stretches. They have the knowledge and skills for the jobs they were hired for, but the context and work demands continue to evolve, stretching these individuals in new (unanticipated) directions. In other cases, people may have been placed in jobs too early with the belief that they would grow into them. Assess the gaps that exist, the situation and context, and focus on how to build the capabilities that people need.

In Amy's case, further conversation reveals that at her previous company she spent most of her time supporting those who were fielding user calls. In that situation, her use of technical jargon was efficient. Your tips should help her move in the right direction.

Attitude issues. People can become frustrated, scared, annoyed, disinterested, or distracted. Other work or personal issues may affect a coachee's current attitude or mind-set toward a particular challenge. In many cases, the person may have the requisite knowledge and skills, but something less obvious is inhibiting his ability to perform. Uncovering the attitude or mental block disabling the person's performance is critical. It could be the setting, or how the person frames or perceives the situation. For instance, someone with strong content knowledge and good communication skills who is quite adept and comfortable interacting or leading discussions in small groups may experience anxiety when he has to apply those same skills in a larger, more formal group. Helping this person think about and reframe the situation in a more productive way, or allowing him to do small pieces first, may provide the confidence needed to perform.

In another case, a person's attitude may be soured and this is holding her back from peak performance. She may feel under-recognized for her achievements, or she may be angry about how the project is being handled and managed, or there may be some other reason. Identifying the source of the underlying frustration or anger is critical to discussing and moving through the situation.

A related but different type of issue is a person who is frustrated or unmotivated because he is fundamentally miscast. The person may be able to get the job done, but at the cost of feeling continually exhausted or frustrated. The gap may not show up in short-term performance, but the effect and drain on the person is noticeable. Understanding enough about the person—likes, dislikes, unique talents, and life aspirations—will help you to decipher if the negative shift in attitude may stem from a poor fit between person and task or role. Let's face it, from time to time people find themselves in jobs that are fundamentally misaligned with what they like and are good at. Helping to surface this and giving the person a safe space to talk it out is important.

Revealing these types of issues requires that you practice your conversation skills—particularly listening, observing, and inquiry— and gently probe to understand root causes.

Resource issues. A person may have the right skills and attitude, but can't translate his or her efforts into performance because he or she doesn't have the necessary time, money, people, or equipment to make it happen. Talking through and identifying the resource gap is critical to resolving the issue. It may be that the resource need wasn't anticipated, or that it was planned for but was unavailable for some reason. Reaching a common understanding of what happened and confirming that the coachee has what is needed before moving forward is an important part of your role as a coach.

Problem framing issues. The problem a person was working on wasn't the same problem you thought that person should be working on. How each of you has framed it doesn't match. For example, Amy may see the user calls as interruptions because she didn't understand the priority those calls have and she has given herself other priorities. Amy is trying to solve the problem of attending to other priorities by rescheduling those technical support conversations with unhappy system users. In contrast, you have framed the problem as "poor support for users" because you saw user support as the top priority for Amy's position, and any other work that Amy is doing should be interruptible.

CHECKLIST

❑ In assessing progress, be sure to use data from multiple sources to get a complete view of progress.

❑ As you engage in giving feedback, remember your conversation skills.
- Be prepared to listen.
- Look for cues that the person is likely to be receptive.
- Ask questions.
- Try to be clear and concise with your comments.

❑ Avoid a tendency to focus *too much* on the past.
- Assess what happened.
- Shift attention toward the next attempt and future results.

❑ Explore root causes and address the issues (capability, capacity, resource) that are actually affecting the coachee's performance.

CHAPTER SIX

PLANNING THE NEXT STEPS

IN THIS CHAPTER

The Planning Conversation ■ Review the Current State ■
Brainstorm the Options ■ Narrow the Choices ■
When You Need to Direct the Action

You may have helped the coachee create goals for future performance. You may have provided some assessment and feedback on his current progress. Although it's important to assess current progress and evaluate *why* the coachee achieved the result he or she did—whether good or not so good—your goal in coaching is to focus on improving your coachee's future performance and results. Therefore, it's important to focus on the future and the next "experiment." Planning the coachee's next steps is a component of the GAPS process. That's where we turn next.

THE PLANNING CONVERSATION

A planning conversation is a chance to consider and plan both what to do next and how to do it. Don't assume that planning for the next step is only important if things haven't gone well. Regardless of how well the coachee has progressed thus far, you should have a con-

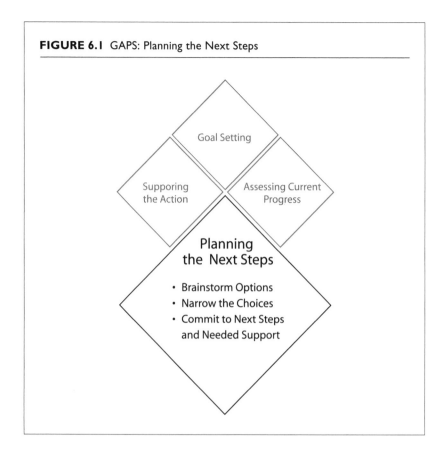

FIGURE 6.1 GAPS: Planning the Next Steps

Goal Setting

Supporing
the Action

Assessing Current
Progress

Planning
the Next Steps

• Brainstorm Options
• Narrow the Choices
• Commit to Next Steps
  and Needed Support

versation to consider the various options going forward and plan for any needed adjustments. The planning conversation may also be combined with other components of the coaching process, such as realigning goals or addressing performance gaps.

When you go into this conversation, keep in mind the need to listen well, to ask questions, to test your assumptions, and to offer your view in a clear and meaningful way. The overall aims are to make sure you and your coachee are *clear* about what has happened and what happens next, to ensure that *accountability* rests in the right place, and to reinforce that the person is *not alone,* that you both are working toward the same desired outcomes. The planning conversation may be brief and compressed into a coachable moment, but needs to happen nonetheless.

A planning conversation typically has three or four components:

1. Review the current state and identify what to work on next (as needed).
2. Brainstorm some possible options.
3. Select criteria for identifying viable options and narrow the options.
4. Decide on and commit to what you both will do—how, when, where, and so on.

REVIEW THE CURRENT STATE

We talked about assessing current performance and results in Chapter 5. If planning is happening separately from assessment, take some time to reflect on progress to date as you plan the next steps. What opportunities has the coachee had to try a new skill or improve performance? What has gone well and why; what hasn't and why? Describe how you each are viewing the current state, and test your assumptions so that you understand the situation in the same way. If there are gaps between the goals and the results, do you agree on the root cause?

Also, if some time has passed since you last discussed progress, you may have additional observations or comments to offer. Taking time to reflect and consider the situation can often reveal additional insights that didn't occur to either of you when previously assessing progress.

During Rasheed's most recent performance review, you communicated that his performance has been very good and that you think he's ready to move into a more senior role within his current work group—a role that either has more direct interactions with clients or is more of a niche product specialist. You asked Rasheed to reflect on what he most enjoys doing, and how his aspirations line up with the potential opportunities you've outlined. As you meet to continue the conversation, several new initiatives have gained momentum and there are even more opportunities for someone with his capabilities.

You:	*Rasheed, when we talked last, I asked you to think about what areas you most enjoy or would be interested in pursuing in the future. I want to reiterate that you are a valuable member of the team and we want to both use your existing talents and make sure that your job continues to be interesting. I'd like to use our meeting time now–the next 20 minutes–to be sure I understand your interests and to make plans for some next steps. How does that sound?*	• Review the last conversation. • Reiterate reason for coaching. • Contract for today's conversation. • Involve coachee.
Rasheed:	*Thanks, I have given it some thought. I have a couple of ideas, and also some questions. I love what I do, but I'm also excited to try some new things.*	• Confirms he's ready for the conversation.
You:	*Great, let's start by talking about what some of the options are. You mentioned you have a few ideas?*	• Invite coachee to start brainstorming.

BRAINSTORM THE OPTIONS

When you both are clear what the situation is and the root cause of any problems, the next step is to consider the alternatives for what to do next. Brainstorming is a way of generating many ideas and thus many potential options that may not be immediately obvious. Part of exploring options includes incorporating ideas based on your own past experience or perhaps ideas from others that you've spoken to in gathering data and feedback.

"Why brainstorm options," you may be thinking, "when I already have a good solution in mind?" For one thing, people have a tendency to embrace the first solution that comes to mind, although it ultimately may not be the best. Rather than simply acting on the first idea, push the coachee and yourself to come up with additional options. Second, your ideas are simply that, your own. Brainstorming allows you and the coachee to express and explore each other's ideas. Ultimately, the coachee is accountable for his or her own progress and needs to participate fully in deciding how to proceed. The exceptions to this approach would be either the case in which the coachee must take certain required steps to turn around a performance problem, or the case in which policy, regulations, or organizational strategy changes mandate specific actions.

A good brainstorming session focuses on new ideas, potential solutions, and the future. It should *not* be used for decision making, or judging and analyzing ideas. Approached with the right frame of mind and done well, brainstorming can be a useful tool. Done poorly, it can hinder rather than help your progress. When the coachee's efforts haven't gone as well as desired, avoid "blamestorming," which has been humorously defined as sitting around discussing why a deadline was missed or a project failed and whose fault that was. Unlike brainstorming, which focuses on the next try and future success, "blamestorming" focuses on criticizing and judging the previous attempt.

If the person is progressing well in meeting goals or in general performance, options for what to do next might include continuing with the status quo, making the goal(s) more challenging, or shortening or changing the learning timetable. You should confirm what you both expect to happen next, which of those general options you're going for, and why you prefer that choice.

If your coachee is *not* progressing well, then you need to generate next step options that specifically address *why* it's not going well. Build off any root cause analysis you may have done when assessing current progress. For example, if the root cause of inadequate performance was a capability issue—the coachee has not had sufficient training or on-the-job experience—then options to address that root cause must include ways of building the necessary capability. Other interventions that you might think of, such as work environment changes or more frequent progress reporting, may also help but won't contribute to building the missing capability.

Brainstorm possible actions you and your coachee can take. Begin the process before meeting, and then extend your ideas as you talk through them together. This is an exploration phase of the conversation, so don't immediately rule out any ideas. This phase of the conversation might go like this:

Rasheed:	*I have a lot of background familiarity with the XYZ client, and it might make sense to move into a more direct role with them. I wonder, though, how my training would work. Also, I'm not sure how I would balance my current responsibilities with new things that I might be doing.*	• Find out what the coachee has been considering.

You:	*XYZ is a possibility. They are a well-established client. They also have a long history with Bill. I think it would be a good area for starting. Bill could take responsibility for your training. We could reduce your current workload to allow you to work part-time with him.*	• Acknowledge his idea. • Offer another option.
	Another possibility is a new client who may be coming on board next month. It would be a little more challenging in that the relationship is just being established, but could be a better fit in the long term. The leader of this project team is also likely to be a senior person who could train you. I can't tell you at this point who that will be. This project will have its own budget, so you would shift there full time and someone else would take over your current responsibilities.	
Rasheed:	*Another idea . . . if there is a possibility of me taking on a more senior financial analyst role, but not working as closely with clients? I think I'm really good at what I do, and I could be a good team leader.*	• Coachee expresses a different area of interest.
You:	*That's an option too. I just assumed you would be good with clients, but you could also be very good at training other analysts. Let's talk a minute about what you like about that role and what the longer-term career prospects might be.*	• Keep all options open. • Brainstorm the second alternative.

Just as you did with the client role option, you and Rasheed brainstorm the senior financial analyst role.

NARROW THE CHOICES

After brainstorming, it's time to narrow the options, and consider which choice(s) best address the current situation and its root cause. In many conversations, you move into this process quite naturally. One key to narrowing the options is agreeing on what the criteria are for including or eliminating them. Decide what criteria you will use to filter ideas, and apply the same rules to all. For example, is this a good first step, is it opportunistic, is it something the person cares about, and is it a capability you want to build?

Coaching is about supporting the coachee; thus, your coachee should take the lead in evaluating and selecting the course of action. As a coach, you should encourage the person to think through the options and evaluate how well each will help the coachee reach his or her goals. This is a point where asking good questions helps guide but not control.

You:	*Of the options we've discussed, what most interests you? What concerns do you have?*	• Focus on the coachee's interest and goals.
Rasheed:	*I am concerned that I may miss what I like about my current role if I choose a project that would move me totally out of that role. Is there a way to explore both more client contact and a more senior financial analyst role? I don't want to make an unreasonable request, but I'm just not sure enough about what I want to do to make a radical change at this point.*	• Combine or compromise options.
You:	*That's a possibility. I understand your reluctance to jump into an unknown role completely. If we can work out the details with two different projects, we might be able to do this. We'll need to find two different projects that are flexible and won't suffer if you later decide it isn't a good fit for you. So, it may not be XYZ.* *Meanwhile, why don't you talk to Bill about his experience when he first did client work. Also, are there any senior analysts you might speak to?*	• Don't make promises about future roles or promotions. • Suggest next steps and encourage coachee to fill in specifics.
Rasheed:	*I understand. I'm open to any projects that could allow me to explore two different areas. And I'll definitely get in touch with Bill, and ask Lee and Tyrone if I can speak with them, too.*	• Coachee acknowledges the compromise. • Coachee takes responsibility and agrees to a next step.
You:	*I'll talk to a couple of my colleagues and see what our project options are. Let's set up a meeting for the week of the 15th.*	• Commit to next steps.

WHEN YOU NEED TO DIRECT THE ACTION

Sometimes, the situation requires more direct guidance from the coach—direction, advice, or suggestions—based on the desired outcome of the coaching. For example, a person who is trying a new skill may not have enough experience to diagnose what's going wrong and why, and to make a good choice about how to "fix" the problem. In that case, the coach as an expert should offer advice about what to do next. Then the subsequent coaching is focused on *how* the person should do the next steps, instead of *what* those steps are.

Narrowing the options entails not only the coach directing action, but also using the opportunity to teach the coachee. So, if you as a coach direct the action, it's important to explain *why* you chose a particular option and why you didn't choose another. Then help the person decide how to go about approaching that option.

Consider what advice to offer, when and in what format, depending on the coaching situation and desired outcome. As you select the right approach, consider also that the coachee may need other resources.

CHECKLIST

The end result of your planning conversation should be to decide what next steps will help the coachee enhance his or her learning, growth, and performance, as well as how and when those steps will happen. Your plan for next steps should be clear, agreed to, and include:

- ❏ *What the goal is.* Restate the desired impact or outcomes.
- ❏ *What each of you will do.* What are the tasks for the coachee and the coach?
- ❏ *How you will do it.* Specific steps or processes to be taken. Also, consider the practicality of the plan. Is it feasible? What management routines, resources, or support is needed?
- ❏ *When you will do it.* What opportunities exist? What deadlines are reasonable? What are the right conditions for the next experiment? What interim steps or check-ins are appropriate?
- ❏ *Potential obstacles.* What could derail the coachee's efforts? What level of involvement is needed from you? What can or should you do to help ease the way or provide a safety net for the coachee's efforts?
- ❏ *Evaluation.* How and when will the two of you evaluate the outcomes of this learning experiment? How will you know if it's working?
- ❏ *Accountability.* What are the implications of success, poor performance, or failure? Are you and the coachee clear about negative consequences or penalties?

CHAPTER SEVEN

SUPPORTING THE ACTION

IN THIS CHAPTER

How Do You Give Support? ■
Show Appreciation ■ Be a Role Model

*"I never teach my pupils; I only attempt to provide
the conditions in which they can learn."*
Albert Einstein, Professor and Nobel Laureate

We have talked about setting goals and evaluating how your coachee is progressing in achieving those goals. We have given an example of what a conversation would sound like when a coach and coachee check in and plan next steps. Another critical component of the GAPS process is offering and receiving support. Ideally a coach is supporting a coachee's efforts all along, but it's especially important after you have established the action plan and the person is preparing to take action.

As a coach, consider what needs to be in place for *this* person to succeed. What does *he or she* need in order to learn, grow, and achieve the results you've both envisioned? Each coaching situation is different, and each individual will have different needs in terms of your support—when, how often, and in what ways: by being a role model,

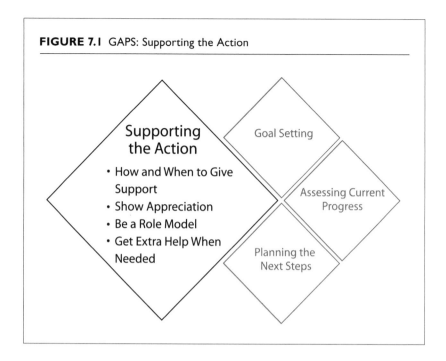

FIGURE 7.1 GAPS: Supporting the Action

showing appreciation for the coachee's efforts, helping the coachee see the possibilities, and recognizing when it's time to get extra help.

As you support someone's efforts, keep in mind the guiding themes we began with. Coaching is a process that happens within a relationship; that relationship should be such that the coach and coachee have good communication and a shared sense of purpose.

Coaches help to create the context and conditions for others' learning, growth, and success. The context and conditions include giving someone the tools and confidence to take the steps independently—and yet you must be prepared to intercede if needed. Your approach should be to stay in touch and be available when needed, but *not* to micromanage. If you observe and measure someone's progress on a regular basis, you are likely to be aware of times when the person needs help before he or she asks. Remember the relationship—coaching is about guiding and teaching, not controlling and grading. The only situations in which your close tracking and steady flow of feedback will be intense are when your coachee is recovering from a serious performance problem or mistake, or when your coachee is working through an emergency situation in which failure would be very costly.

HOW DO YOU GIVE SUPPORT?

Coaching is about creating the conditions for success, and a critical piece of success is the support that coachees receive during the process. The amount of support they require will depend on the type of outcome the coaching is targeting, the amount of gap that exists between their goals and current performance, and their individuality. Each situation and coachee will be unique. If they are attempting something that is a natural extension of their current capabilities, their need for your support will likely be less. On the other hand, if they are attempting something that they anticipate will be extremely difficult or intimidating, be prepared to provide more active support. Either way, you should supply more than "good luck" and a hearty pat on the back.

For example, when a youngster is first learning to swim, parents often climb in the pool with the child or put inflatable "water wings" on the child's arms. The parent's hands or the water wings help the child float and keep his or her head above water. These help make the child feel safe while learning. When the child's skill improves, the parents no longer bring out the water wings and let the child swim unaided for longer periods. They stay close by and monitor the child, but they offer less and less direct teaching and support.

When the child later learns to dive into the water, the amount of learning is reduced and the amount of support he or she requires is minimal. The child already understands the basics of swimming, and is just extending existing skills. However, if the child wanted to become a competitive diver or learn to scuba dive, additional training, support, and supervision would be needed. The parents would likely decide that they also need the help of external "coaches" to guide them through the process or to take over. Just like with the water wings, the coach would offer support as the budding diver learned to do twisting, turning dives; the coach would likely attach a harness and have the diver practice on land (on a trampoline) to learn the dive's motions, before advancing to diving in the water. As the diver's skills improve, he or she might go on higher diving boards or add another half twist or somersault in the air. His or her efforts to learn and perfect those skills, though, have a coach behind them.

"Big day, Haskins. The training wheels come off."

As you support your coachee during this process, take care of the relationship and remember that the primary outcomes are the individual's learning and development. The following tips offer some suggestions for how you can provide support.

- *Act in ways that maintain trust.* You are there to help. Make it clear to your coachee that it's safe to admit to you if he is struggling with a task, not really understanding what to do, or having doubts about his ability to reach the goal. Even if he has agreed to coaching, it may take time for the person to trust you enough for your coaching to truly be effective. For example, Rasheed has been helping out with senior financial analyst duties the past few days because they are shorthanded. He's getting some great experience but seems a bit overwhelmed at times. Let him know that this particular job has a high learning curve and you expected him to experience some difficulties, but you also know that he is very capable. Encourage him to talk with the other analysts and to also come by and chat with you after he's had a few more days in the department.

- *Make it a point to check in.* Acknowledge any difficulties and successes so that together you can decide how to proceed. Check-ins, like coaching meetings, can be brief or more formal. Opportunities for checking in happen naturally—a quick debrief in an elevator in the minutes between meetings, during a phone call or lunch away from the office. A quick check-in is fine as long as the coachee has other opportunities for more time when needed. For example, you run into Chris as you're leaving the office. He notes that the new project team is just getting started, and that he's attended a management fundamentals course and was really energized by the instructor. He's tossing around the idea of returning to school—maybe not for a degree but perhaps just more short courses. You encourage him and suggest checking out tuition assistance possibilities. You also make a mental note to schedule more time next month after the project is well underway.
- *Identify where the coachee most needs support and consider whether routines would be helpful for that situation.* Routines can help provide structure, remind people what they need to do, facilitate learning through repetition, and keep skills or tasks in context. Tips:
  - Keep the routine as simple as possible. Don't have 17 steps if 5 really will do. Too many steps will be harder to learn and may generate more confusion than help.
  - Keep the routine as regular as possible. If there is a report due weekly, have it due the same day each week (e.g., each Tuesday).
  - As the person's skill level changes, consider revising the routines. Once the person has mastered the basics, you might add in steps or vary the way in which the person accomplishes the tasks.

    Establishing routines can probably help Amy with some of her communication gaps. You don't think she fails to communicate on purpose; she just gets focused on other things and forgets. Routines around *how and when* to communicate might include:
  - Sending a revised update schedule to all teams and their leaders each Monday.

- Sending a detailed plan to her team members and manager one week prior to the actual date.
- Performing all updates on Wednesdays as that is the least disruptive day.

- *Teach or demonstrate what they need to learn in a way that is most beneficial to them.* You can do this directly by instructing or more subtly by being a visible role model. Keep in mind that people have different learning styles, and you may need to tailor your approach to better match the ways in which your coachee best receives and retains instructions—listening to you talk through the information, reading a reference guide, watching someone else, hearing an example or story, or jumping right in and giving the task a try. No one uses a single style exclusively; there is typically some overlap, but people have definite preferences. Observe and ask what works best for that person. For example, Chris is getting direct on-the-job exposure to other areas of the company through his new project group, and getting training through his fundamentals class.

- *Let the person know that you are there if he or she needs assistance.* A coachee needs to know that you are both available and approachable. The person is likely to be aware of the number of existing demands for your time and may be hesitant to add something else to your list. If necessary, be creative in finding ways to make yourself available. Just like training wheels on a bicycle, knowing that you are available *if* he needs you is sometimes all that's required. Use the quick check-ins to reiterate when you're most available and how to best contact you (voice mail, e-mail, your assistant, and so on). Also, let the coachee know what times are bad, so he or she knows when you really can't be interrupted.

- *Partner with the coachee to solve issues or get resources from beyond your area.* The coachee may occasionally need access to or support from other coaches, other experts, or other areas of the organization. This may include access to information, formal courses, equipment, or opportunities. Be prepared to use your own network to help extend another's support network.

- *Be prepared to intercede when needed and remove potential obstacles.* Creating a safe environment for learning includes providing "air cover" and protection as your coachee experiments, and being prepared to run interference if necessary. (Politics can be an obstacle to someone trying a new skill.) Part of being a supportive coach is giving someone the time and space to try, fail, and try again. In some cases, it may be giving the person some privacy while trying.

Be cautious when putting someone into situations that might require your intervention. If you do need to intervene, do it in a way that doesn't undermine or denigrate the person's efforts. For example, a manager was leading his first big project, while at the same time he had other smaller projects to work on. At one point, the client turned to his boss and said, "This guy isn't meeting our needs." It was an important client, and the boss needed to intervene in a visible way; she apologized to the client, saying the manager was overloaded and she would find additional resources to reduce the burden. This made the client happy—they'd get more attention—without undermining the manager—the number of projects was to blame. She then paired the manager with a more experienced colleague who could coach the manager on how to handle a big project, as well as offer some tangible help to get the work done.

SHOW APPRECIATION

What do we do when we show appreciation? We recognize, acknowledge, and show that we understand the nature, quality, or magnitude of someone's hard work and effort, even if the results aren't complete and her performance can still improve. We can also appreciate and empathize with someone when things don't work out at all as intended, because perhaps we've been in a similar situation.

Appreciation is about the person—his or her efforts and learning—not always about performance. In Chris's case, you may acknowledge the fact that he has stepped outside of his normal comfort zone and is experimenting with a new role on a project team, as well as taking responsibility for getting additional training.

Support isn't reserved for a coachee who is struggling with a particular goal or trying to improve performance, and appreciation isn't reserved for those who are experiencing total success. Both are necessary in the learning process. *All individuals need to understand that you are observing and aware of what they're doing, that you understand their efforts, and that it matters.*

Show appreciation by:

- *Tailoring appreciation to the individual.* Acknowledge that people have different needs, tolerances, and expectations about levels and forms of appreciation. Use your knowledge of your coachee and your relationship to determine how and how often to offer positive reinforcement. If you don't know what the coachee will respond best to, then ask.
- *Being honest.* Overstating your praise can make people feel patronized and can send the wrong message about how you really feel about their performance. Ultimately, that type of feedback isn't helpful and it could damage your coaching relationship.
- *Encouraging them to recognize their own effort.* They may be so focused on results that they fail to appreciate how hard they are working toward their goals or how much progress they're making.

BE A ROLE MODEL

Your role as a coach is both direct and indirect. As a coach, you directly and explicitly help someone learn a new skill and offer answers to specific questions. However, you also act as a role model for others; your coaching is indirect in these cases. Those you coach may look to see how you behave or how you do a particular task. They might imitate your actions as they experiment and learn. They look at your attitudes to make sense of the organization's culture and decisions. As a leader, you should model the environment you are trying to develop. Coaching is a way to develop individual competencies and performance but is also a method of translating and fostering the culture that you want to create.

Consider Mother Teresa, a woman who built a network of schools, hospitals, and homes for the poor. The culture in her order was of hard work and doing for others. She slept on the floor and routinely worked 16-hour days. She taught school, ministered to the sick, and built an organization filled with women who followed her example of service and humility. She embodied the culture she wanted to create and asked nothing more of others than what she herself would do. You likely manage fewer people than Mother Teresa did, but they look to you and your example.

CHECKLIST

❏ Are the coach's mind-set and coaching culture being reinforced?
  • You are there to help.
  • Everyone has something to learn.
  • The coachee's learning and development are the primary goals.
❏ Are you completing the entire coaching process cycle?
  • Are you helping them set SMART goals or look beyond immediate goals to future aspirations?
  • Are you giving them timely and constructive feedback on their efforts thus far?
  • Are you helping them plan appropriate next steps to achieve their goals?
  • Are you supporting them through each of these steps?
❏ When needed, are you accessing the additional support that they need? Such as:
  • Other coaches
  • Resources
  • Training
  • Role models

CHAPTER EIGHT

THE CHALLENGING CASES

IN THIS CHAPTER

The Resistant Coachee ■ Coaching to Address Personal Efficacy ■
Coaching a Peer ■ Coaching Upwards ■
Getting Extra Help ■ Keep Coaching and Learning

On its face, coaching seems to be a straightforward process: build a relationship, follow the basic process outlined in GAPS, use communication skills well, and away you go. Unfortunately, the experience won't always flow that smoothly. At times coaching is a challenge. Sometimes it's a challenge because you don't have the skills or experience to be effective or a situation takes you by surprise. Sometimes it's a challenge due to your relationship (or lack thereof) with the other person. Sometimes the challenge stems from the uncertainties about the appropriateness of coaching those who don't report directly to you. Other times, the challenge is cultural, if success in the organization is defined as "knowing" the right answer rather than "learning" the potential answer. (Senge, 1994) Sometimes, you don't intervene because you just don't think that you have the right to do so.

In this chapter, we explore four types of challenging cases—when the coachee is resistant, when the coaching needs to address personal efficacy, when the potential coachee is a peer, and when someone who's higher up in the organization needs coaching. All of these cases may require both an added degree of courage and refinements to your coaching approach.

THE RESISTANT COACHEE

You are trying to help, but you feel like you're talking to a brick wall or shouting into the wind. You and the coachee agreed to a set of goals, but he or she isn't working on them. You offer advice, but the coachee won't take it. You jointly made a plan, but the coachee only seems to be going through the motions. In spite of your best efforts, you feel you're not effective with a particular person. If you sense the person you are trying to coach is resisting your efforts, it's important to understand why. The resistance may be related to his or her personal preferences and views, it may be related to you as manager or coach, or it may be related to the prevailing situation in the organization.

Resistance may be rooted in the coachee's personal preferences and views in any of these ways.

- *Arrogance.* In spite of performance data, the coachee doesn't think the issue you've pointed out is a weakness, and doesn't see a need to change.
- A *blind spot.* The other person doesn't recognize the development area or need for change that you see.
- A *deep-seated part of his or her self-concept.* The behavior you think needs to change is deeply connected to the coachee's sense of self, and therefore he or she is reluctant to accept counsel.
- *Workload.* With all his or her other demands, the coachee doesn't see the value in spending time working on the improvement area you have targeted.
- *Fear.* The coachee doesn't trust you enough to reveal a weakness.
- A *misconception.* The coachee has never been coached and equates coaching with personal failure.
- *Discomfort.* The coachee would rather learn on his or her own (discomfort with the method), or the coaching outcomes are

outside the coachee's comfort zone (discomfort with the development area).

It may not be *you* specifically that the coachee is resisting, but rather the approach of learning through coaching. Resistance may also be rooted in the coachee's opinion of the manager or coach in one of these ways.

- *Perception of manager's capability.* The coachee doesn't trust your capability, doesn't view you as an expert on the subject or as an effective coach.
- *Perception of manager's availability/workload.* The coachee may feel he or she is intruding on your time.
- *Perception of accessibility.* The coachee may feel that you aren't easily approachable—that you seem "too smart."
- *Manager's attitude/treatment of coachees.* The coachee finds you arrogant, disrespectful, or intimidating.
- *Preference for alternative coach.* The coachee would rather be coached by someone else—he or she admits a weakness but doesn't think you are the right person to help with it.

Resistance may be related to organizational issues, such as:

- *Not part of the organizational culture.* Performance questions are equated with a (usually negative) evaluation.
- *"Sink or swim" culture.* The attitude may be that if you can't succeed on your own, you are never going to make it here, or that getting help is a sign of weakness.
- *Overly risk-taking culture.* People believe they can "go it alone" because the culture encourages unwise experimentation.
- *Lack of resources.* Coachees know that resources are not available to support coaching, or to support safe experiments, and so they feel that responding to coaching is a waste of time.
- *Not a learning organization.* A premium is placed on execution and "getting it right" the first time.

How do coachees resist? Resistance can manifest itself many ways. The coachee:

- *Doesn't show up at the meeting.* The person resists scheduling a coaching session or skips it.
- *Doesn't engage during the coaching conversation.* He or she doesn't listen, withdraws, or nods but doesn't interact.
- *Resists afterward.* The coachee fails to follow through, never quite keeps commitments, or follows the "letter of the agreement" but shows no energy, enthusiasm, or deeper commitment.
- *Turns down offers of coaching.* The coachee says "It's okay; I've got it," or claims to be unavailable.

What to Do

First, try to understand the underlying reason for the resistance. Recall Amy, the newest member of your IT support team and a recent hire from outside the company. You know already that she has problems with communication—both receiving and giving. As well as being introverted, she is also very task focused, to the extent that she can simply forget to communicate important information to others. Why might Amy resist coaching? There are many possibilities. Perhaps her previous organization did not value coaching and she is finding it hard to adjust to a different culture. Perhaps she finds coaching conversations too personal, intrusive, and unwelcome. Maybe she finds it hard to trust others and prefers to work out problems on her own. Perhaps she simply has not yet managed to "hear" the message that you would like her to make some changes in the way that she works.

After uncovering the underlying reason for resistance, get your ego out of the way and consider whether you really are the right coach for this person. Consider whether you might be contributing to the person's reluctance and what you might change in your own approach. Ask the coachee if there is someone else with whom she would be more comfortable, and take steps to match her with another coach. In Amy's case, this might be a peer of yours, a more experienced peer of hers, or someone who has recently made a successful transition into the company.

Finally, make sure the issue is appropriate for coaching. Is it about a behavior that interferes with the employee's successful performance or simply one you don't like? Is it about results, or is it about your need to control the method of achieving results? Is it about a different mind-set, or is it about a mind-set that conflicts with yours?

If you conclude that you are the right coach and the issue is appropriate for coaching, then you may need to get creative.

- Focus on establishing a good relationship with the person, so that a trusting foundation for coaching is laid. Invest more time than you have so far.
- Ask someone you respect for input and suggestions. This might be your own coach or mentor, or it could also be someone outside work whom you trust to keep the conversation confidential.
- Talk, in confidence, with a former boss of the coachee, to see how he or she provided coaching.
- Schedule regular conversations with the coachee and talk more broadly about your own developmental path, mistakes you have made, insight you have gleaned—especially in the area where you think he or she needs guidance. If you choose this route, you will need to check carefully whether your elliptical suggestions have been acted on.
- Declare a "dead, stinking moose under the rug" conversation—an unusual conversation whose ground rules are to be candid, to lift the rug, and openly talk about the "problem" that got swept under there. What does that mean? In any social group, we sometimes find ourselves tip-toeing around known but not discussed issues: everyone knows that the company is going to have layoffs, but no one mentions it; everyone thinks that a certain director is incompetent but they all work around him. Sometimes, the way past a problem is to call it by name and say, "We keep avoiding this and it's not going away. Let's talk about it." If your coaching relationship is stalled and you can't figure out why, framing it as a "moose" conversation may give the person permission to say what the real trouble is.

- Persist gently. Let the coachee know you're available if and when he or she is ready to talk.
- In some cases it is both appropriate and more effective to escalate the issue. Make it clear to the individual that this will become a performance issue unless he or she addresses it—and you are there to help the coachee to do so.

COACHING TO ADDRESS PERSONAL EFFICACY

In most of this book, the coaching needs are related to performance—poor performance, new performance, developmental performance. A different kind of coaching challenge has to do with the employee's sense of self, identity, competence, or efficacy. In other words, people who have been performing adequately or even very successfully, but don't see themselves as competent, or feel overwhelmed, or doubt that they will accomplish anything. Perhaps they are overworked and frustrated; perhaps they are perfectionists with unrealistic standards; perhaps they are so involved in the day-to-day grind of work that they can't see their accomplishments and progress. Whatever the reason, the issue that the manager needs to address is the sense of self-efficacy that underlies actual performance competence. Sustaining and improving this sense is critical to ensuring the person maintains his or her performance and results.

Take the example of Chantal, a project manager in an engineering firm and a member of your program team; you are her program director. Chantal communicates well with the clients, she keeps her project team motivated and delivering on time, she negotiates successfully with vendors and keeps the project within budget, and completes her own design assignments. You sit down with her for her annual performance review and goal setting meeting, your feedback is strongly positive, and your only concern is whether the amount of time Chantal puts in every day is putting her at risk of mental burnout or physical illness.

Chantal does not respond with energy or enthusiasm. You finally point out her low energy and ask for her view of the year. She describes herself in comparison to your most senior project managers and a couple of program directors, pointing out how little she accomplishes or can handle compared to what they do. She goes on to describe how she feels she has to put in long hours to just keep up with the work, and half the time she's convinced it isn't really up to expectations. She seems to focus on small errors and minor mistakes, and she attributes successes to the team or lucky circumstances.

At this point, you may be thinking that Chantal's situation is beyond your capabilities to address and may be more of an emotional or personality problem rather than a "work" problem. Before you settle on that conclusion, consider the possible causes and review the tips below.

Reasons for self-efficacy issues can include:

- *Unrealistic performance standards.* A new person may expect to perform at the same level as experienced peers, or a junior person may try to match the performance standard of a much more senior person. A perfectionist may be unwilling to accept the chaos, messiness, disorganization, and imperfections of complex, dynamic processes with multiple, changing stakeholders. Someone successful in a different environment in a previous position may be expecting instant success in a drastically different new environment. A consistently independent employee may avoid asking for advice or more resources when faced with a more demanding assignment.
- *Loss of perspective.* Someone deeply involved in the daily detail of a long-term project or assignment may lose track of the bigger picture and become focused on the frustrations, delays, or small errors of the moment. That person may become unable to recognize the overall accomplishments and progress.
- *Lack of capability.* Employees who have been promoted, put on a stretch assignment, or given new jobs without adequate preparation and training, may assume that the uncertainties, doubts, and missteps they experience are their own "fault." They may assume that whoever provided the work "knew" they were capable of performing it, and so become frustrated or overwhelmed by any signs of ineffectiveness.
- *Lack of capacity.* Although managers know that individuals have different capacities depending on their capabilities and

experience, and different tasks or assignments have different demands, sometimes they misjudge or misallocate work. Such employees can end up with more to do than they should be expected to handle, but if they assume that their workload is "normal," they may begin to question their competence or fitness for the position.

- *Lack of effective or efficient tools or routines.* The person may be trying to get work done with tools or management routines that are ineffective or inappropriate. This situation could be as simple as using a paper-based method when software is available or as complex as ineffective delegation or resource allocation. With ineffective tools or routines, the work becomes overwhelmingly time-consuming, and if the employee concludes that the inefficiency is his or her "fault," the employee may become discouraged, self-critical, and self-doubting.

- *Poor "fit" between the person and the work.* Sometimes people end up doing work that does not match their interests or make good use of their talents and experience. If such employees feel powerless to make a change because of organizational barriers—no openings, no precedent for the necessary change—they may become discouraged and frustrated, doubting their ability to continue contributing to the organization.

- *Lack of development or unmet aspirations.* One of the most important nonfinancial rewards of working is the sense of growing, moving ahead, or learning new things. Sometimes, typically for structural reasons, organizations fail to provide adequate employee development or fail to pay attention to employees' aspirations, which can lead some of them to question their value and feel discouraged about their options.

What to Do

The first step is to acknowledge that there is a problem or a concern. Sometimes when a manager faces a problem with an employee that seems personal or not amenable to analysis or rational understanding, it is tempting to either ignore it in hopes it will somehow get worked out or expect the employee to have a "stiff upper lip" and push through. So admitting that there might be a problem with the individual's sense of personal efficacy is essential.

The next step is to acknowledge the situation with the individual, who may also be tempted to ignore it or try to push through it. Having acknowledged the situation, the third step is exploring what's going on and why. The kinds of areas to explore include:

- *Expectations.* Was the coachee led to expect something that was not delivered? Does the coachee have unrealistic expectations of himself or herself, of the job, or of the organization?
- *Structural issues.* Was there insufficient preparation or training for the assignment or job? Is the workload unrealistic? Is there inadequate development or career opportunity for what the coachee needs and wants?
- *Perspective.* Has the coachee had a chance to step back and review the bigger picture of his or her work over time, recent work in comparison to past work, or work in comparison to typical performance by others? Is the coachee overly focused on recent delays, frustrations, or mistakes?
- *Capability development or resource needs.* Does the coachee need to learn new skills? Does he need to learn new techniques, routines, or processes? Should the coachee have more efficient tools?

As you explore one or more of these areas, you may need to expand the individual's perspective with your own input or with feedback from others. Sometimes it is helpful to recount stories of the personal efficacy challenges that you have faced or with which others have struggled, pointing out either the pain or difficulty of the situation and describing how the person overcame it.

Finally, you should address the coachee's point of view. Some personal efficacy issues arise or are made worse when the individual's perceptions are not true. For example, a coachee may tell herself that no one else is struggling and she is the only one; she may tell herself that there's nothing she can do to change the situation; she may believe that the difficult situation is "the way things are supposed to be." In any case where you hear, explicitly or implicitly, someone expressing a point of view that is not necessarily true but is interfering with his or her ability to take effective action, point out the alternatives. When you take this step, your empathy and good communication skills will be especially important, because you will be touching on areas related to personal identity and outlook.

If your coaching conversations suggest that your coachee needs support and guidance beyond your capabilities, take advantage of whatever resources your organization offers to get advice for yourself and help for the employee. Seek out your HR professional, a more experienced manager, or an employee assistance program.

COACHING A PEER

Peer coaching is unique. It is the relationship in which the mutuality of coaching is most obvious. In other words, with your peers, you can easily be both the coach and the coachee. You may develop a relationship that is mutually supportive, where you experiment and grow alongside a colleague. In this way, you can create a safe space where learning is fun, as you cover for each other and try out new things. However, it is important to ensure that the relationship stays reciprocal and does not grow closed to input from others in the organization.

As your colleagues' peer, you are in a position to understand well what they are experiencing because you likely have similar pressures, similar challenges, and similar relationships within the organization. You often can be a good coach to your peers because you are not in their chain of command and because you are more attuned to where a peer may be having trouble. Similarly, your peers are in a good position to understand what you need and to give you coaching from outside the management structure.

Peer coaching is also unique because a peer is simultaneously a colleague and a potential competitor. For many, giving feedback to or receiving feedback from a colleague is uncomfortable and sometimes risky. If the relationship is friendly and trustful, a peer can be very helpful giving you advice and network connections just as you can be helpful to your colleague. However, if the peer sees you as competition for resources or a promotion, or you see him or her as a competitor, then asking that peer for advice or coaching, or offering advice or guidance, requires more caution.

More often, though, people can grow and develop from peer coaching. It can be less threatening to reveal a weakness to a peer—there is a sense that this person understands the issues deeply, and it's seen as an exchange of favors. Peers tend to be effective in learning from one another's experience.

What to Do

Although some peers are quite willing to give advice and counsel, they may not be as eager to receive coaching and instead see it as an attack. Take an informal approach to discover whether coaching is needed and welcome, and whether they consider you an appropriate coach.

- Build relationships to the point that you feel comfortable sharing your concerns or challenges.
- Issue casual invitations—acknowledge a problem and wait. The person is free to pretend not to have heard or to decline the invitation to talk.
- Ask permission. Name an issue and offer to help: "It seems you have a problem with _____ . I don't know if you remember, but I used to do a job like that. Want to have lunch and chat?"
- Be clear if you're having a complaint session or a problem-solving session. Even among friends, it helps to contract.
- Tell a story about yourself. For example, "I used to have difficulty with this or this happened to me one time and here is how someone helped me."
- If you receive coaching, be prepared to reciprocate.

In some cases you can't be delicate. For example, if someone violates company culture or ethics, or harms someone else, you have a duty to respond. As a member of the community, you can and should raise the issue and help coach or enlist an appropriate coach for that peer. As before, you need to use effective communication skills, offer feedback in a way that the person can hear and support the person's efforts to change or to correct a misstep.

COACHING UPWARDS

Everyone needs coaching. Many people realize this. However, in the executive ranks it has become almost fashionable to have a private coach. These coaches can be effective, but should not be the only ones giving the executive feedback and advice. There is a time and place for people (including you) to get coaching from a subordinate. Just like your direct reports, you and your boss need feedback as to how you are doing.

It is often sensitive to give advice to someone who is higher in the hierarchy. You may not be seen as credible, the person may react badly to a perceived criticism, or the person may "shoot the messenger." For these reasons and others, people often don't offer their perspective. However, one of the time honored routes to success is to find ways to help someone senior to you perform well and come across to others in the very best light. If you can find a way to coach your boss or some other senior person, the rewards can be great.

Finally, your general concern for others and for the success of your department, group, or organization can motivate you to look for ways to tackle the challenging task of coaching upwards.

What to Do

We discussed showing appreciation to your people. You should also offer positive feedback or appreciation to your boss. If that person handled something skillfully or gave you more time than he or she really had, or if you found a piece of advice useful, tell the person. Let your boss know what's working well. People in more senior positions may *seem* to need it least, but can benefit greatly from appreciation for their efforts.

Likewise, there may be areas where your manager isn't handling a situation well. If you do offer negative feedback, keep it limited. As before, ask yourself whether the feedback is important and appropriate, and whether the person can or will do something about it. Address only one or two issues at a time, and test whether the person will be receptive.

- Ask if a suggestion would be useful.
- Connect the feedback or the constructive suggestion to the senior person's strength or valued goal.
- Make it seem as if the senior person came up with the idea (or at least pointed the way toward the idea).

Remember, you can't be useful—to your boss or your people—if you get fired. As always, consider whether you are the right person to act as coach or whether you should work indirectly through another person.

GETTING EXTRA HELP

If you are facing some coaching opportunities that are more challenging than the usual, recognize the limits of coaching as well as your own limits as a coach.

- Don't try to use coaching to address a factor in the individual or in the organization that you can't change.
- Coaching is neither psychotherapy nor a personal help line. Maintain the coaching relationship, but recognize when people need additional personal support, or when *you* need assistance with special situations. Factors that fall outside the bounds of work may be inhibiting the person's capabilities and having a negative effect on his or her performance. You can't ignore these factors, but you may not be the right person to address them.

If you feel your coachee needs something you can't provide, refer that person to someone who can, or encourage him or her to seek appropriate help independently.

Be sure you:

- Address performance issues, even if you suspect they're caused by off-the-job problems.
- Make it possible for your subordinates, team members, and colleagues to acknowledge that personal situations are having

an effect on work, without necessarily having to go into detail about what the situations are.

- Know what resources your organization has for helping employees who are having difficulties outside work. Have contact information handy.
- Consult with more experienced managers and appropriate groups within your organization if a coachee is having problems beyond your skill or comfort level.

You don't want to:

- Ignore signs of personal problems.
- Probe for personal details.
- Tell someone to "just get a grip."
- Press other coworkers for private information.

KEEP COACHING AND LEARNING

Perhaps you have begun a coaching relationship and successfully navigated through the coaching activities of goal setting, progress assessment, planning, and support. There may have been some glitches or you may have encountered some of the challenging coaching situations, but you and your coachee are working through the process and have experienced some success. Congratulate yourselves, and then keep going.

For both the coach and the coachee, coaching is a dynamic, creative, and cumulative experience. Each learning opportunity and success builds on the previous one and prepares you for the next one. The coachee continues learning, developing, and growing in capabilities, and the coach continues enhancing his or her ability to offer coaching and support. As you progress through a coaching relationship, or work through challenging coaching situations, return to these guiding principles to help you and your coachees continue to make progress.

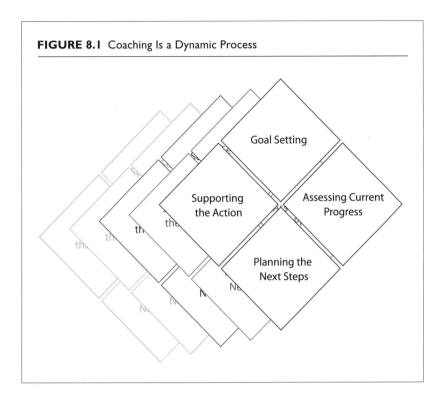

FIGURE 8.1 Coaching Is a Dynamic Process

- *The relationship is the foundation.* Your relationship should allow you to have honest, productive conversations. When the relationship is threatened, take time to restore goodwill.
- *The goal is learning and self-sufficiency.* Increasing the coachee's capabilities, performance, and confidence is your goal, and you share responsibility for the outcomes. Your expectations about what your coachee can achieve and your desire to help are critical to his or her success.
- *It's a team effort.* Continue to monitor the *conditions* for success, adapting resources, creating new opportunities to experiment, providing feedback, and offering support. In turn, the coachee should continue to act on the goals, incorporate feedback, and seek and use support.
- *Keep the right focus.* Connect and recognize the benefits for the individual, manager, team, and organization as the coachee continues to make progress. Especially in challenging situa-

tions, don't forget to ask if coaching is the right approach for this individual at this time.

- *Keep it going.* You may make mistakes. Learn from them, but keep going. Remember, imperfect coaching is better than no coaching at all. As you improve your own coaching skills, consider how you can help others learn to be better coaches, or help your organization to improve the coaching culture.

BIBLIOGRAPHY

Buscaglia, Leo F. 1984. *Loving Each Other.* New York: Ballantine Books.

Entre Nous. 2005. "Mentoring Profiles." Canadian Youth Business Foundation. http://www.mentoringyoungentrepreneurs.com/ EntreNous/index.cgi?p=MentoringProfiles&s=&#M8 (accessed March, 2005).

Fisher, Roger, and Allan Sharp. 1998. *Getting It Done: How to Lead When You're Not in Charge.* New York: HarperCollins Publishers.

Fiske, Susan T., and Shelley E. Taylor. 1991. *Social Cognition.* 2nd Ed. New York: McGraw-Hill.

Flaherty, James. 1999. *Coaching: Evoking Excellence in Others.* Boston: Butterworth-Heinemann.

Fulmer, Robert M., and Marshall Goldsmith. 2000. *The Leadership Investment: How the World's Best Organizations Gain Strategic Advantage through Leadership Development.* 1st ed. American Management Association.

Gaines, Lynn. 1995. "Your Work Stinks!" *Executive Female.* May/ June, Vol. 18, Issue 3, 42.

Goldsmith, Marshall. 2002. "Try Feedforward Instead of Feedback." *Leader to Leader,* no. 25.

Goldsmith, Marshall, Laurence Lyons, and Alyssa Freas. 2000. *Coaching for Leadership.* San Francisco: Jossey-Bass/Pfeiffer.

Harvard Business Essentials. 2004. *Coaching and Mentoring: How to Develop Top Talent and Achieve Stronger Performance.* Boston: Harvard Business School Publishing.

Hunt, James M., and Joseph R. Weintraub. 2002. *The Coaching Manager: Developing Top Talent in Business.* Thousand Oaks, CA: Sage Publications.

Infinite Innovations Limited. 2003. *Brainstorming Definitions.* http://www.brainstorming.co.uk/tutorials/definitions.html (accessed 2005).

Krzyzewski, Mike, with Donald T. Phillips. 2001. *Leading with the Heart: Coach K's Successful Strategies for Basketball, Business, and Life.* New York: Warner Business Books.

Maister, David H., Charles H. Green, and Robert M. Galford. 2000. *The Trusted Advisor.* New York: Touchstone/Simon & Schuster.

McLeod, Angus, Ph.D. 2003. *Performance Coaching.* Carmarthen: Crown House.

Rosenthal, Robert, and Lenore F. Jacobson. 1968. *Pygmalion in the Classroom.* New York: Holt, Rinehart & Winston.

Senge, Peter M., et al. 1994. *The Fifth Discipline Fieldbook.* New York: Doubleday.

Starcevich, Matt M., Ph.D. 1999. "Coach, Mentor: Is There a Difference?" *Center for Coaching and Mentoring, Inc.* http://www.coachingandmentoring.com/Articles/mentoring.html (accessed 2005).

Stone, Florence M. 1999. *Coaching, Counseling, and Mentoring: How to Choose & Use the Right Technique to Boost Employee Performance.* New York: AMACOM.

Seuss, Dr. 1990. *Oh, the Places You'll Go!* New York: Random House, Inc.

Weinstein, Harold P., Ph.D. 2005. "Mentoring, Coaching, and Performance Reviews: Clarification for Managers." *Bostonworks.com.* http://bostonworks.boston.com/nehra/041105.shtml (accessed 2005).

Whitmore, John. 1992. *Coaching for Performance.* London: Nicholas Brealey Publishing.

INDEX